THE BEST PLACES YOU'VE NEVER SEEN

The Pennsylvania State University Press
University Park, Pennsylvania

THE

BEST
PLACES

YOU'VE

NEVER
SEEN

PENNSYLVANIA'S
SMALL MUSEUMS
A TRAVELER'S GUIDE

THERESE BOYD

Contents

Heart of the Alleghenies

Iron City Environs

Heading for Lake Erie

Top of the World

While digging up the small museums of Pennsylvania, I often found myself saying, "What is a small museum?" "Where is it?" Why is it . . .?"

"Small museum." The Metropolitan in miniature? What exactly does a small museum encompass? These words mean different things to different people, but in my travels I have come to believe that pretty much anyone can slap up a "Museum" sign on a building (and even, sometimes, get along with no sign at all) and some unsuspecting traveler will wander in off the road.

But that doesn't make it a museum.

"Museum" conjures up an image of a large building. The Carnegie in Pittsburgh, the Franklin Institute in Philadelphia, the State Museum in Harrisburg. These places are well advertised and heavily visited. But who has heard of—or seen—the Wharton Esherick Museum in Valley Forge? Bill's Old Bike Barn in Bloomsburg? The Toy Robot Museum in Adamstown? We also have a Wild West museum, a number of music museums, even a museum dedicated to the shoe. Pennsylvania is full of these little wonders.

Large museums are often created with corporate money or substantial private endowments, have curators, executive boards, and swanky fundraisers. Buildings may be designed with a particular genre in mind. Small museums are not always planned—they happen, maybe in the corner of someone's house, or a storefront, or an old building no longer serving a useful purpose. If they have a "board," it often means a husband and wife are in it together. "Fundraising" can mean an admission charge or merely a jar by the door labeled "Donations."

Large museums house "important" items, great works of art, some famous person's belongings. Little museums contain someone's heart and soul. Most often they start out as a collection that just got out of hand. A couple in Hanover had (until not long ago) an ice cream museum. They still own the materials but for some reason wanted to reclaim their house. Sorry I missed it.

Other small museums are attached to companies—a room or two or an entire building—to commemorate an industrial history. The Marx Toy Museum in Erie was put together by former employees to showcase their dedication to the Marx Toy Company. I had the pleasure of visiting it, and fully intended to include it here, but later found it had closed up shop. Too bad.

Large museums take life and art very seriously, in hushed surroundings, with dim lighting and a closely monitored thermostat. But how seriously can one take a collection of carnival glass and spittoons that fills one small room in Breezewood with lit glass cases of multicolored wonder? Given a choice, I'll take spittoons over fruit-bowl still lifes any day, but that's the kind of hairpin I am.

Some small museums do feature a more serious side of life. The final stop on a tour of the African-American Museum in Reading is the closet trap door beneath which runaway slaves hid from their pursuers. A tour of any coal mine in the state will bring mention of a cave-in, how many miners died, what "black lung" is. Museums can feature a life, either a person's—like the George Westinghouse or the Wharton Esherick—or a company's—such as Piper Aviation or the Yuengling Brewery.

How did I come to choose these forty-two places out of the hundreds of small museums in Pennsylvania? I tried to find the unusual and the unknown, those places with little or no budget for advertising, yet worth a stop. I tried my best to represent the entire state. Small museums are best found through word of mouth (how we found the Toy Robot Museum) or by stopping on a whim at the sight of a rotating, pasty-white weightlifter, destined to hoist his barbell forever in front of the Bob Hoffman Weightlifting Museum and Hall of Fame.

Locating the museum itself could be an adventure. I often drove around a while, sometimes even clutching a brief set of directions. When a friend and I looked for one museum in a small central Pennsylvania town, it didn't seem to be at the address we had. We stopped a man on the side of the road to ask for directions, but he said he hadn't heard of it. He then called his wife over to help. When I said the name, she turned and pointed next door: "There it is."

What makes a "good" museum? I've found that to be totally in the eye of the beholder. Someone who had been there told me not to bother with the Mushroom Museum in Kennett Square; I found it interesting (but smaller than its own gift shop). My husband would have been bored stiff in the New Holland Band Museum, but the musician in me loved it.

Digging up these museums wasn't always easy. Knowing

that some once existed but are no more was disappointing. Like the ice cream museum, both the Streitwieser Foundation Trumpet Museum and the Norman Rockwell Museum closed before I ever had a chance to visit. A lot of places are open only by appointment or have unpredictable hours. Sometimes phone aren't answered regularly. But, just as often, someone is nearby who will be glad to open the door, to invite the traveler in for a look.

Of course, I tried to make this book as accurate as I could. Each museum owner/guide did his or her best to help me, but there was an awful lot to be absorbed. I suspect there may still be errors and, if so, they are solely my own.

It seems as I continue this exploration, I find more and more museums that no one has heard of and yet, as soon as I describe what I've seen, my friends want to see them as well. *The Best Places You've Never Seen* are some I've visited. If you know of a little museum not mentioned here, one that you think I might have missed, send me an email at smallmuseumsofpa@aol.com. More are yet to be discovered, I'm sure.

List of Symbols

free Admission is free

$ Admission is $5.00 or less

$$ Admission is more than $5.00

Gift shop on the premises

Handicapped accessible

Kid friendly

Restrooms available

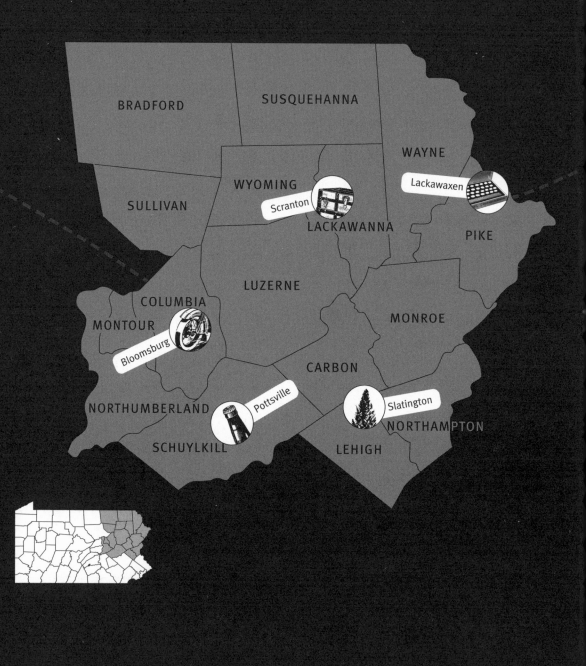

BRADFORD

SUSQUEHANNA

WAYNE

WYOMING

Scranton

Lackawaxen

LACKAWANNA

SULLIVAN

PIKE

LUZERNE

COLUMBIA

MONTOUR

MONROE

Bloomsburg

CARBON

NORTHUMBERLAND

Pottsville

Slatington

NORTHAMPTON

SCHUYLKILL

LEHIGH

BETTER IN THE POCONOS

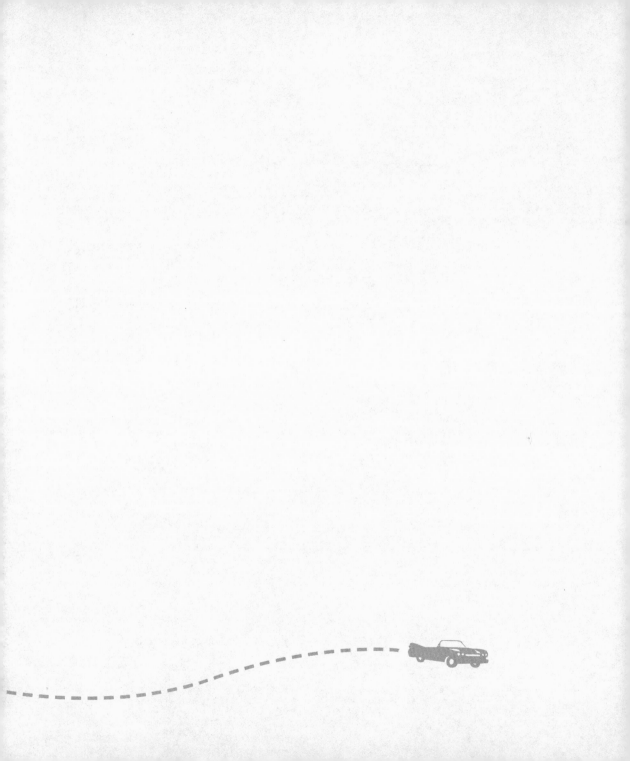

Bill's Old Bike Barn

It seems the Harley-Davidson plant has *always* been in York. And it has always had a plant tour and a vintage motorcycle display. So why did I head north to Bloomsburg? While as of this writing the plant is still in York, the Harley Museum has moved to Milwaukee. Now, if you want to see vintage Harley-Davidson motorcycles in Pennsylvania, you've got to go to Bill's Old Bike Barn.

And that's where I went, singing "Gitcher motor runnin'" the whole time. I've ridden a motorcycle exactly twice in my life (sorry, Mom), both times as a passenger. I loved it. I understand completely the magnetism these machines have, the feeling of freedom while riding. For some people, nothing beats riding a motorcycle. And some will tell you, if it ain't a Harley, it ain't a motorcycle.

Thankfully, Bill's Old Bike Barn isn't that restricted. Bill Morris has worked with motorcycles for over thirty years and, with the help of his girlfriend, Judi Laubach, opened the museum two years ago to house his personal collection.

One sunny Saturday afternoon, I followed the driveway up behind Bill's Custom Cycles to the large museum building at

the top of the hill. A few motor-cycles, including one with a side-car, sat out front. Obviously, these bikes were being used. On my way to the door, I crossed in front of a large cage, from which a parrot kept a close and wary eye on me.

Judi started my tour by explaining how the building was put together. Judi and Bill and a group of friends found four barns within twenty miles of Bloomsburg. Each barn was dismantled—"the women pulled out all the nails"—and then "the men put them back together" into one structure. Now the museum is two large rooms, with walkways on a second level in both rooms. More than just Harleys, this is a tremendous display of bikes, collectibles, and other stuff that just caught their fancy. I don't know how else to explain the carousel horse or the sixteen-foot-tall tin knight from Mexico, found in an antique shop in Wilkes-Barre.

Don't call them bikers, Judi said. "We're enthusiasts." I think that's an understatement. To describe the motorcycles alone would be difficult. The 1913 Silent Grey Fellow is the oldest bike in the collection. But I also saw a 1937 Indian Chief, a 1937 Knucklehead, a 1949 JD with sidecar, and a 1961 Moto Guzzi—and that wasn't even half of the collection. The Guzzi is Italian; Bill says he particularly likes Moto Guzzis and plans to put more on display. I saw cute little

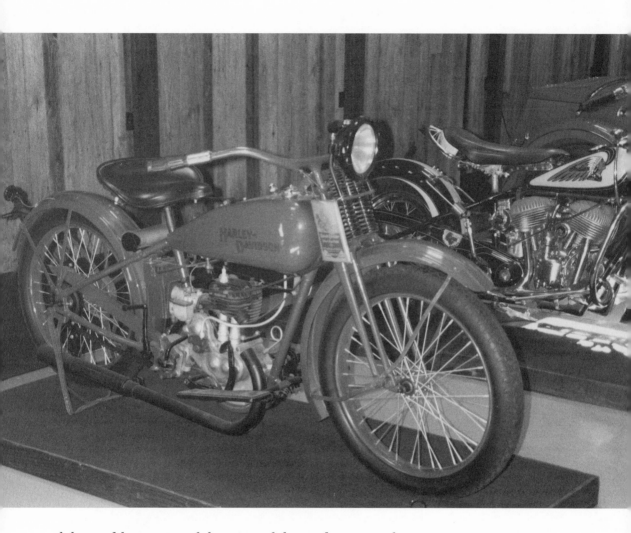

A 1949 Hydra-Glide Harley.

bikes and big monster bikes, Army bikes and a 1941 police bike, bikes in all colors and sizes.

I would venture to say they have every single Harley collectible ever made, but I had no idea most of these things existed, so maybe I'm not a good judge. But I saw beer

Bill's Old Bike Barn

7145 Columbia Boulevard
Bloomsburg, PA 17815
(570) 759-7030
www.billsbikebarn.8m.com

HOURS:

Tuesday–Friday 1 A.M.–6 P.M.
Saturday 9:30 A.M.–3 P.M.

DIRECTIONS:

From I-80, take Exit 241, Bloomsburg, and go north on Route 11
one mile. The museum driveway
is just before Bill's Custom Cycles
on the left; the museum sits up
behind the shop.

steins, playing cards, model planes, trucks, cars, glasses, plates, watches, flasks, pins, key rings, ashtrays, an HO-scale train, Christmas snowglobes, bells, taffy, wine, coffee, bracelets, hats, boots, golf balls, and stamps. Then, of course, there are movie posters, gasoline signs, and beer ads, spread out all over the museum in glass cases. And I'm sure I didn't see everything.

Items directly motorcycle related: oil cans and parts boxes and different motors. Harley gave each motor a name, such as "panhead," "shovelhead," and "knucklehead." You can even push a button to see one of the motors operate. Bill told me that future plans include adding a "Wall of Death" to the interior of one of the spiral staircases. If you're unfamiliar with the Wall of Death, you've never been to a county fair.

Even with all these things, I didn't feel overwhelmed in this museum. The rooms are arranged well and the tour is self-guided so visitors can wander to their hearts' content. Bill and Judi added some of the nonmotorcycle items when they realized that nonenthusiasts had little to do while the enthusiasts were touring. Judi said she kept hearing, "I'll wait in the car." Now, with things like the 1939 World's Fair memorabilia and the wicker motorcycle, noncycle people are more likely to stay.

While Bill doesn't exactly bring the words "He's a rebel" to mind, his disagreements with the Harley corporation are legendary in motorcycle circles. He told me these days Harley is "like McDonald's," that every franchise has to be the same as every other. He supports individuality in bike shops. And his museum is clearly a monument to that independent streak. Gitcher motor runnin'. . . .

Houdini Tour and Show

Houdini. In *Scranton, Pennsylvania*? I had to find out why.

More than seventy-five years after his death, Harry Houdini is still regarded with respect and fascination by many. His life and death were full of mystery and secrets. A magician and showman, he died tragically and—some say—by someone else's hand. In our minds he will forever be as handsome as Tony Curtis, who played him in the movies.

But why is "the only museum in the world devoted totally to Houdini" located in Scranton? What was the connection? Had Houdini once escaped from a mine? Had he been an Irish miner in a previous life? I know he didn't live long enough to risk his life driving among the tractor-trailers dominating I-81.

But that's precisely what I did. One hot Saturday afternoon I found the museum tucked among homes on Scranton's north side. Once I located the right neighborhood, I couldn't miss the building, painted light blue, with sideshow-style paintings of rabbits and Houdini on the street-level walls, and dressed Houdini-like mannequins standing on the second-floor balcony with a large advertising banner.

"FAILURE means a DROWNING DEATH!"

—Houdini

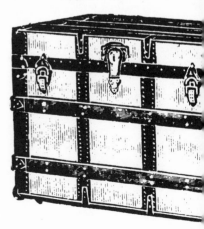

Loud and lively music was playing as I stepped into the dark front room and paid my admission. I slipped into a seat in a crowd of about twenty people. Before our eyes, magicians Dorothy Dietrich and Bravo the Great (a.k.a. John Bravo or Dick Brooks) did sleight of hand and other magic tricks, as well as some standup comedy, pulling audience members on stage to participate as needed. The patrons—more than one a Houdini fan—loved it.

After the show, we saw a short film of magician Doug Henning doing Houdini's Metamorphosis trick (two people exchanging places in a locked box) and then were given some time to wander around the front room, adjusting our eyes to the light while the children bought magic wands and other tricks. Finally, we were taken on a tour of the History Room and the Prop Room, in the back of the house. Which you see first—magic show or tour—depends on the time you arrive.

Every piece in the museum is a tribute to Harry Houdini. The walls in every room are covered with framed posters from his shows, as well as collections of padlocks Houdini used. Silent films that Houdini made with his own production company fill video screens when the magic show isn't on.

In the History Room, Houdini's life is displayed in pictures and text. Erik Weisz, the man who would rename himself Harry Houdini, was born in Hungary in 1874. His family moved to Appleton, Wisconsin, where his father was a rabbi, before moving to New York City. (Appleton has a museum, too, but it only has one section on Houdini.)

Houdini started his magic act at the age of seventeen. By the time he was twenty he was married to his life-long partner, Bess (Janet Leigh to you movie fans). At the turn of the century, having become successful in the United States, Harry and Bess moved to Europe and became international stars.

The "King of Handcuffs" gradually moved to escaping from larger items. The ultimate showman, he added aspects of danger and thrill with such acts as leaping off a bridge while manacled and freeing himself underwater. He accepted challenges regularly from people inviting him to escape from contraptions they had devised.

The Prop Room contains some actual items from Houdini's life, both personal and professional, such as padlocks and handcuffs. The pictures of his parents that originally hung on the wall of his home now hang in the museum. The straitjacket on display was used by Houdini's brother, Theodore Hardeen, who continued as a magician after his brother's death. Ominous black letters on a large milk can—a staple of one of Houdini's escape acts—reminds visitors of his promise: "Failure Means a Drowning Death."

Houdini was famous for exposing spiritualists as frauds. He testified before House and Senate subcommittees considering a bill to prosecute fortune-tellers. When other magicians started copying some of his tricks, he published a book outlining ways to escape handcuffs, taking the mystery out of their work. (His own work had developed beyond

Houdini Tour and Show

1433 N. Main Street
Scranton, PA 18508

(570) 342-5555
www.houdini.org

HOURS:

Call for specific hours. Weekends in June, every day in July and August. Halloween show through October.

DIRECTIONS:

Take I-81 to Exit 190, the Main Ave Exit (old Exit 56). Go left exactly 2 miles to 1433 N. Main Ave.

such simple tricks.) They also tried to compete with him by calling him a fraud but he continually proved them wrong.

The Houdini legend lives on. Bravo and Dietrich, who have collected Houdini memorabilia for years, originally displayed their collection in their Magic Townehouse at 61st Street and Third Avenue in New York City. They moved to Scranton in 1993 after crime in New York hit too close to home.

When the two magicians aren't operating the museum, they tour and perform at schools and corporate events. Some of the few non-Houdini items in the museum are clippings highlighting Dietrich's career as a magician and her skill at catching a bullet in her teeth (a trick Houdini reportedly refused to do).

I learned much about Harry Houdini that I didn't know. He invented a deep-sea diving outfit that a diver could escape from. He made five silent films. Houdini was the first person to fly an airplane in Australia. When he toured, Jack Benny was his opening act.

And that's where Scranton comes in. Houdini appeared at the Polis Theater in Scranton more than once in his career. According to John Bravo, it was a major stop on the vaudeville circuit, just before New York City. Then nearly the big time, Scranton, Pa., is now the home of the only museum in the world totally devoted to Harry Houdini.

White Christmas Chalet and Tree Farm

⊙ **Slatington**

Some people believe a museum should make a visitor think. The White Christmas Chalet and Tree Farm made me do more than think—I downright wondered, pondered, and questioned. What the heck do sleds and Christmas have in common with minerals, Indian artwork, butterflies, and potatoes?

Seems self-explanatory from the name, doesn't it? A Christmas tree farm with some added attractions. My friend Joyce and I followed the careful directions and the can't-miss-them white Christmas tree signs out of Slatington and up a hill. We came to the large wooden building that is labeled "White Christmas Chalet." So far, so good.

Then we walked inside. The foyer had display cases on the walls with large rocks. It looked more like the mineral section of the Smithsonian than a Christmas scene. We entered the main room. There was a larger-than-life Santa Claus, standing next to a horse-drawn sleigh. Back to Christmas. But behind Santa, the wall to the left was lined with more minerals and rocks, along with some fossils.

We were puzzled but curious. The Chalet is often used as

a reception hall for weddings; caterers were setting up during our visit. While we waited to talk to Bertie, who manages the Chalet, we wandered into another room full of Christmas items. We found ethnic religious iconography, including a Black Madonna, and a fraktur from 1879. When I saw the Infant of Prague standing in front of Santa candy molds, I began to think our host might be Catholic.

From there we entered the Vista Room, where windows on three sides provide a full view of the valley below. The walls right next to the ceiling were lined with children's sleds through the years, fifty years' worth, from 1870 to 1920. We saw a cannonball skeebob, a monobob, and a dog-drawn Canadian sled. More sleds adorn other parts of the building, covering the next fifty years until 1970, but the ones in this room were the oldest.

About this time Bertie joined us. She explained that the museum was started by the tree farm's owner, Grant White, and is an assembly of his interests. While the museum tour is self-guided, with an accompanying booklet, Bertie showed us through the museum personally and explained some of the pieces. She shook the sleigh bells and told us how the sounds of different bells were distinctive enough that neighbors knew who was passing by. She modestly said she didn't know a lot about the pieces, but she could answer every one of my questions.

I asked about the eclectic nature of the collection and Bertie told me I would have to meet Mr. White. While she went off to find him, Joyce and I wandered some more. In the Northern Lites room, we found Indian dreamcatchers and statues. Another room contained a case of toys relating to Christmas, as well as a case of Santas. We walked outside to find displays about limestone, sandstone, and potatoes ("How the Potato Changed History"), as well as an enormous conch shell, a wildlife display, and a small walking path through a variety of Christmas trees.

Bertie called us back into the building to meet Grant White. His description in the guide booklet, "An educator and naturalist who received the first degree in environmental education awarded in Pennsylvania," may be accurate but it doesn't do him justice. Grant is a very interesting man,

White Christmas Chalet and Tree Farm

3072 High Hill Road
Slatington, Pa 18080
(610) 767-0177

HOURS:

Seasonal in fall and winter.

DIRECTIONS:

From Route 22, take 309 North to Route 873. Turn right on Old Post Road and left on High Hill Road. The White Christmas Chalet and Tree Farm is at the top of the hill.

with more interests than there is time in the day to pursue.

For openers, he told us, "Christmas relates to everything." I had never thought about it. He told us that, in the nineteenth century, thirty-two different religions came through the port of Philadelphia and that Christmas celebrations really took hold after the Civil War. And I was wrong; despite the Infant of Prague, he isn't Catholic but he's very interested in religion. He sees Christmas as more than Christian. According to the tour booklet, Christmas is "celebrated through yearly rites and rituals rooted in both the spiritual and social needs of people and the annual cycle of nature." Hence, the rocks and other natural items.

Even the art on the walls has more story to it than it may appear. We looked at framed *Saturday Evening Post* and other magazine covers with winter scenes. Grant pointed out enthusiastically that these were not photographs but drawings and paintings from before photography was commonly used on magazines. He pointed to small details in the art, such as a child standing in a doorway, and said, "That can't be shown in a photo." Never occurred to me.

If you visit the White Christmas Chalet and Tree Farm, walk slowly and look around. Grant told us that he wants to excite the intellectual in visitors and said, "Museum doesn't mean 'dead.'" I couldn't agree with him more. In this case, you'll be thinking about all the things that you've seen long after you leave.

Yuengling Brewery

It was a Wednesday in November. The weather was inviting enough, warm and dry. But I still didn't expect thirty adults of all ages on a 1:30 p.m. tour of the Yuengling Brewery. Some were locals, obviously with a day off. Others had traveled from as far as Minnesota (land of Pabst, to hear them tell it). Only six were women, and none of those without a man.

We had all climbed the hill in Pottsville with one thought in mind: *beer.* We were about to tour "America's Oldest Brewery." The younger members of our group thought this was hallowed ground. They don't remember when Yuengling was "your dad's beer," something you stole out of the basement refrigerator but never drank if you had another option. Now younger generations have made Yuengling Black & Tan a popular choice at trendy establishments—not what you'd expect coming from the coal-ravaged hills of Pottsville.

Yuengling has both a plant tour and a museum. I started with the plant tour since it's only given at certain hours. We were led into the Hospitality Room, a small dark-wood bar next to the museum, which was originally built so that the

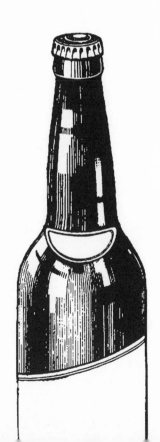

OUR MOTTO
PURITY
CLEANLINESS
D. G. Yuengling & Son.
BREWERS & BOTTLERS
POTTSVILLE, PA.
ESTABLISHED 1829
ELEVATOR
WAGON SHED
BOILER HOUSE
STABLE
COLD STORAGE
MALT HOUSE
D.G. YUENGLING & SON.
SHIPPING DEPARTMENT
OFFICE
MASH TUB
KETTLE
ELECTRIC LIGHT PLANT
STABLES
YUENGLING'S PARK

workers could quaff one on breaks or at lunch (hold off on that application form—it's no longer allowed). Our guide, Melanie, gave a talk on the brewing of beer and the history of the company. I didn't learn any company secrets, but it was very interesting.

In short, David Yuengling, a German immigrant, started his brewery in Pottsville in 1829. When the building burned down two years later, he moved the shop up the mountain to its present location. The land was more desirable because it contained a cave where Yuengling could store beer at a constant 42 degrees. We were disappointed that we couldn't see the cave; our guide said the floor was too slippery (or "slippy" if you're from Central Pa.). As it is, you must wear closed-toe shoes for the plant tour, and rubber soles are a good idea.

The brew for all Yuengling beers follows the same path from a stainless-steel cereal cooker, through to the mash tun (think big covered vat), lauter tun, and brew kettle. The sign reading "Caution. Caustic" on the brew kettle didn't seem to bother anyone in my group, but it made me wonder what was particularly lethal. Every batch of brew makes 450 barrels, or 198,288 12-ounce bottles. Almost enough for a fraternity party.

After the stillness in the kettle room, the commotion in the bottling room was a jolt. We felt the soapy spray as we walked past the tall brown long-neck bottles being cleaned. During filling and capping, the bottles clanged against the metal machines, making my ears ring. The heat from the pasteurizer (which holds 10,000 bottles) warmed our faces as we peered into its little windows to see all those rows of bottles

OPPOSITE: The Yuengling Brewery hasn't changed much since this depiction was drawn over a century ago.

17

Yuengling Brewery Museum

Fifth and Mahantango Streets
Pottsville, PA 17901
(570) 628-4890
www.yuengling.com

HOURS:
Monday–Friday 9:00 A.M.–4:00 P.M.

TOURS:
Weekdays 10:00 A.M. and 1:30
P.M. Saturdays only in June, July,
August, and between Thanksgiv-
ing and Christmas, 11:00 A.M., 12
P.M., and 1:00 P.M.

RESTRICTIONS:
Closed-toed shoes only. No sandals, flip-flops, or any other
shoes with openings (front, back,
and sides). Call to make arrange-
ments for group tours.

DIRECTIONS:
From Scranton/Wilkes-Barre, take
I-81 south to Frackville/Saint Clair
Exit. Take Route 61 south to
Pottsville (7–8 miles). Take a right
(continued on opposite page)

lined up. On another day we might have seen cans being filled and capped, but I knew I wasn't missing a thing.

During the tour we followed Melanie, walking up and down narrow metal stairs, through the room with the kettles, over wet floors, outside, up a hill, and back down. So many companies these days keep a great distance between a tour group and real plant operations. Not at Yuengling. We walked among the brewery workers. We saw real ingredients and actual beer-making machinery up close. Although every-thing is very clean, this is not a shiny, ultra-modern, high-tech facility. You don't need to look farther than the old wooden door labeled "hop storage" to remember that Yuengling is a very old company and deserves its spot on the National Register of Historic Places.

The company is currently run by Richard Yuengling Jr., the fifth generation at the brewery. His four daughters are now working to preserve the family tradition and will some-day purchase the company from their father. One of my tour mates was horrified to learn that women might actually be able to run a beer company. Sounds like he needs his own cave.

Our forty-five-minute plant tour ended back in the Hos-pitality Room, where samples were poured and tasted. I could tell which tour mates had been to a tavern before; they were the ones leaning an elbow on the bar while watching Melanie pour from the tap. (Yuengling also serves birch beer for the non–beer drinker.) After my tasting, I went into the room next door, Yuengling's museum and gift shop.

As you might imagine, family history plays a big role at this brewery. On display in the museum are photographs of all five generations of Yuengling owners and the building over the years. Except for the horse and carriage out front being replaced by trucks, you couldn't tell whether the year was 1850 or 1950.

Brewery tools, such as a bung tap and a keg bung remover, are on display. Historical business records include a receipt book and a brewing book from 1903. The beer-bottle and beer-can exhibits are complete and labeled by years. How many types of beer collectibles have been produced? I counted fourteen: glasses, mugs, cans, signs, ads, bottle labels, caps, can openers, pens, ashtrays, calendars, key rings, taps, and coasters. I may have missed some. But you don't have to. Turn around from the displays, walk ten feet, and you can buy whatever your collection needs.

The tour is self-guided and the museum is in the same room as the gift shop, so although tour times are limited, you can visit the museum anytime the gift shop is open. This place is a beer fan's dream: see it made, taste it, and take home some souvenirs. The only way it might be better would be if they sold takeout. But—this is Pennsylvania, after all—you'll have to find a beer distributor in Pottsville instead.

on Norwegian Street (next to Century 21/Ryon Realty). At the next light (two blocks), take a left on South Centre. At the next light (one block), take a right on Mahantongo. D.G. Yuengling's is four blocks on the left. From Harrisburg, take I-81 north to the Ravine Exit. Take Route 125 to Route 209, and follow signs to Pottsville (12–13 miles). At the Pottsville city line, Route 209 turns into West Market Street. At Fourth Street, turn right. D.G. Yuengling's is two blocks on the right.

Zane Grey Museum

"Lack-a-waxen." Just rolls off the tongue, doesn't it? This tiny town is tucked into the northeast corner of Pennsylvania (literally—it sits on the Pa.–N.Y. line). Cities melt away up there into mountains, forests, and creeks. A lot of people vacation in the area—think "Poconos"—but I made the trip just to see the Zane Grey Museum.

I didn't know a whole lot about Zane Grey before my trip. To be honest, I wasn't too excited about a museum dedicated to the "Father of the Western Novel." But it was a beautiful summer day and I enjoyed the drive. I passed a sign for the Dancing Bear Country Hippie Emporium, but much to my disappointment it was only "Coming Soon." Then I passed the Shady Rest Hotel, but it was closed down. (I guess Uncle Joe really had moved too slow.)

Finally, I came to Lackawaxen and the Zane Grey Museum on the western bank of the Delaware River. This National Historic Site is the house Zane Grey bought with his brother, R.C., in 1905. Zane and his family lived there from 1914 until 1918, when they moved to California, but they maintained the house for years and came back often.

According to the park ranger on duty, twenty to thirty people a day tour the house in the summer months. More than that come inside to the gift-shop section but don't care to spring the $2 for the tour (probably the same ones who drive around Yellowstone taking pictures of geysers without ever leaving their Winnebagos). But I didn't drive all that way not to plunk my $2 on the counter and ask for the complete tour package!

Jared Gricoskie, a National Park Service intern and Penn State Rec/Park major, was my guide. He had only been working at the museum for about a month and wasn't yet confident of all his information, but he gave me a great tour. I learned that Zane Grey was far more than just the Father of the Western Novel. He was also a baseball player, dentist, and avid fisherman.

Pearl Zane Gray (he would later drop the "Pearl" and change the spelling of his last name) was born in Zanesville, Ohio, in 1872. Multiple careers ran in the family: his father was a preacher, farmer, and dentist. Zane grew up hunting, fishing, and playing baseball, and when he was old enough, he helped his father by pulling patients' teeth, which was the main dental treatment at the time.

While Zane was known as a skillful tooth-puller, patients still complained about his lack of a degree. He had no real future without one, so he enrolled at the University of Pennsylvania on a baseball scholarship. Academics were not his strength, but it seems he had one heck of a curve ball. Zane played baseball in the summer, went to school the other months of the year, and managed to graduate with a degree in dentistry in 1896.

21

Once he was out of school, Zane pursued his first love and played in the minor leagues for two years. But when the rules changed and the space between the pitcher and the batter was lengthened, his curve ball—and baseball career—went south. He then combined a successful dental practice on Central Park in New York City with fishing on the banks of the Upper Delaware River with R.C. It was there twenty-seven-year-old Zane met the young woman who would have the greatest impact on his career.

Ten years younger than Zane, Lina "Dolly" Roth came from a wealthy family. Her master's degree in English from Columbia University came in handy after she and Zane married, when she became his editor, agent, and biggest supporter. Zane's writing career started small; his first article, "Day on the Delaware," published in 1902, netted him only $10. The following year, with more encouragement—and funding—from Dolly, he self-published his first novel, *Betty Zane*, complete with his own artwork.

Soon, though, things took off. Zane started traveling with Col. J. C. "Buffalo" Jones. Together they toured the Grand Canyon and from that trip came his first real Western work, *The Last of the Plainsmen*. Many more novels followed, some made into radio shows or silent movies. The Grey family moved to California in 1918 so that Zane could oversee the production of his work, but they returned to Lackawaxen regularly over the years.

Zane's life would be the envy of many. After he wrote the first draft of a novel, Dolly would do whatever editing was necessary, find a publisher, and negotiate the best deal with that publisher, all the while raising their three children.

"**LOVE, STRUGGLE, WORK, CHILDREN**— all came to us there."

—Zane Grey,
writing to Dolly about visiting the house in Lackawaxen.

Zane Grey Museum

Route 590 (Lackawaxen Pike)
Lackawaxen, PA 18435
(570) 685-4871
www.nps.gov/upde/zgmuseum.htm

$ 🛍 ☺

HOURS:
June–August, Wednesday–Sunday
10 A.M.–5 P.M.; May, September–
October, weekends 12 P.M.–4 P.M.
Limit 10 people per tour.

DIRECTIONS:
From Route 6 turn north on Route
434. At Greeley, go left on Route
590. Once you're in Lackawaxen,
you'll see the sign to turn right for
the museum.

THE BEST PLACES YOU'VE NEVER SEEN

When Zane wasn't writing, he was traveling to research his next work, not hiding the fact that he often had female travel companions.

By the 1920s, Zane's career struggles were over and he began to spend much time pursuing other interests. An avid fisherman, he was the first man to catch a 1,000-pound abigone with rod and reel. In all, he netted ten world angling records. He dreamed of fishing the Seven Seas, but the Depression intervened, and he had to come home to California.

Zane Grey died in 1939, having completed 120 books and manuscripts. Until her death in 1957, Dolly made sure to publish one of his manuscripts every year, thereby helping to keep his name alive. The genre he helped create lives on in Western books and movies. A modern magazine of Western stories bears his name.

And Lackawaxen never left Zane's shadow. When Dolly sold the house in 1945 to a friend of the family, it became the Zane Grey Inn. The new owner collected Zane Grey memorabilia and opened the Zane Grey Museum in 1973. In 1989 the National Park Service purchased the property. In addition to summer tours, they open the museum the last weekend in January to celebrate Zane's birthday. The Zane Grey's West Society (www.zanegreysws.org) holds talks in Lackawaxen during that weekend as well.

The guided museum tour goes through the first floor of the house, what was Zane's office and studio. The room is decorated with Navajo-style paintings by Dolly's cousin. Jared led me past artifacts from Zane's youth through his numerous careers, including his dental tools, which made this dental-phobe wince. I was much happier looking at the books, manuscripts, and artwork—the art both Zane's and Dolly's. Between Jared's narration and all the photographs, I was caught up in the life of Zane Grey. He wasn't perfect, but he was certainly interesting.

In that shady, window-lined room it's not hard to envision Zane sitting in his chair (he didn't use a desk), creating his stories while looking out over the banks of the Delaware River. Even today I can see why he loved it—it is a beautiful, peaceful spot. Worth the long drive.

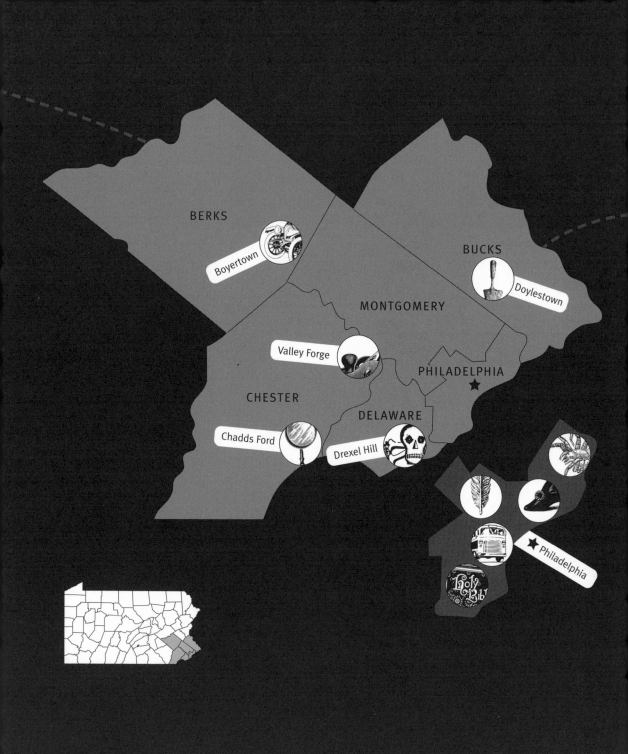

BERKS

Boyertown

BUCKS

Doylestown

MONTGOMERY

Valley Forge

PHILADELPHIA

CHESTER

DELAWARE

Chadds Ford

Drexel Hill

Philadelphia

AROUND THE CITY OF BROTHERLY LOVE

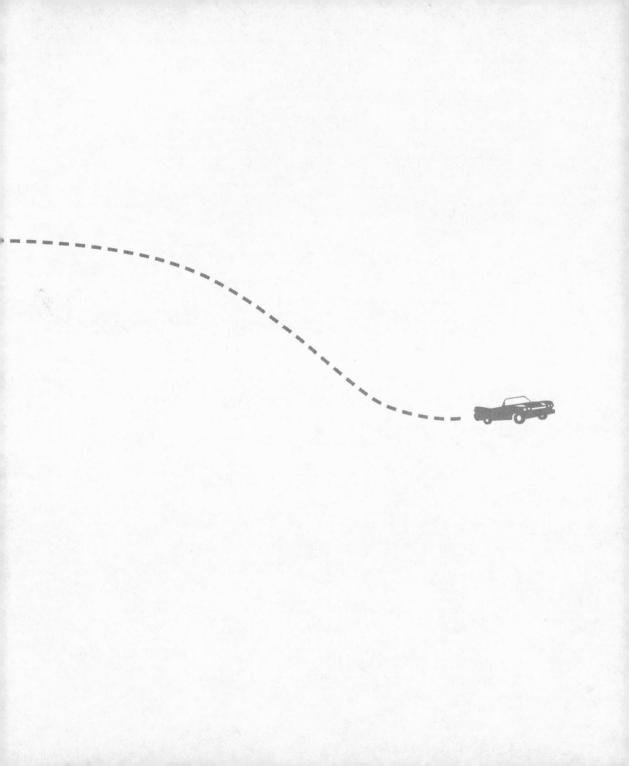

Boyertown Museum of Historical Vehicles

Pennsylvania was never a threat to "the Big Three," and no one will ever say "Reading, Pa." in the same way they say "Detroit." But we've had a significant number of car manufacturers, especially in the southeastern part of the state. Ever hear of Daniels? Fleetwood? Duryea? Some of these were independent and some were related to other better-known companies. But they were all Pennsylvania car makers.

Before the horseless carriage, there was the horse-*with*-carriage and the Jeremiah Sweinhart Carriage Factory in Boyertown. Once the age of the automobile began, the carriage company became the Boyertown Auto Body Works, which lasted until 1990. Paul Hafer, the Body Works' CEO, started the museum in 1965 to recognize Pennsylvania's special place in automobile history. Until 2002 the museum was housed in the original factory buildings. But space there was too tight to hold the growing collection of cars, so the museum moved just a few blocks away.

I assumed that I would see mostly cars, but the museum lives up to its "historical vehicles" name. The tour begins with a collection of sleighs, including a two-horse bobsleigh

Motorheads might call this Duryea a "three-banger" (it has three cylinders).

from 1905, a doctor's buggy that looked straight out of *Gunsmoke* ("He's hurt purty bad, Doc, you better come quick"), and a real live surrey with a fringe on top— consider that last one your cue to sing. I guarantee you won't be the first. There are even bicycles and baby carriages.

One of the museum's highlights is the "world's largest" electric car collection. Electric cars are not a late-twentieth-century environmentalist idea. By 1900, 40 percent of the cars on the road were electric. The uniquely named Electro-Bat was built in Philadelphia in 1895. Even Mrs. Henry Ford drove a 1914 Detroit Electric, a gift from Thomas Edison; the museum owns a 1919 Detroit similar to hers.

This sojourn filled in the gaps in a fascinating story I'd heard growing up. My family often visited the Pagoda, the little red building on top of Mount Penn in Reading, former-hotel-now-tourist-destination. The narrow winding road from Reading's City Park up to the Pagoda can be treacherous. I had been told more than once that the road was a test track for Charles Duryea's cars. In fact, the road is now named Duryea Drive, in honor of this Pennsylvania car maker. But that's as far as the story ever went.

In the museum I learned that Duryea—already a car

maker with his brother before coming to Reading in 1900—formed the Duryea Power Company. He is credited with developing the first gasoline-powered car and being the first to use inflatable tires. In Reading, Duryea built one three-cylinder car a week, selling each one for $1,250 to $1,600.

Although each car was made carefully, Duryea wanted to be sure they would work. So he developed what he considered a reliable test. Duryea's daughter, Rhea, would drive the new car from Reading's City Park to the Pagoda in high gear. If she made it, the car was sold. If she didn't, the car was worked on until it could make that trip.

Despite Duryea's achievements, and the fact that his cars were tested so thoroughly, his car business failed in 1907 and again in 1914. But his work lives on in the museum. We looked at a 1904 Duryea Phaeton and a 1908 Buggyaut. True to its name, the latter looks more buggy than car, but it was very versatile and could be used as a pickup truck or passenger vehicle. I guess you could call it the first SUV.

One of the few pieces in the museum with no Pennsylvania connection is a two-horse hearse from England, ca. 1870. With its glass and silver lamps, silver coffin holder, and Waterford crystal windows, it is an impressive sight, although it brought to mind the ghost hearse running up the stairs in *A Christmas Carol*.

Some visitors are only going to want to look at the surface of the cars—the paint, the hubcaps, the upholstery. Others will surely prefer their "inner beauty"—the engines, gears, and drive shafts, pulleys, belts, and cylinders. Each car has a full explanation of its mechanics as well as its personal history, so there's something for everyone.

Boyertown Museum of Historical Vehicles

85 S. Walnut Street
Boyertown, PA 19512-1415
(610) 367-2090
www.boyertownmuseum.org

HOURS:
Tuesday–Sunday 9:30 A.M.–
4:00 P.M.

DIRECTIONS:
From the Pennsylvania Turnpike, take Route 100 north to the Boyertown Exit, Route 73. Turn left at the top of the ramp and drive through Boyertown. At Route 563, turn left. Go two blocks to Third Street and turn right. The museum is a block and a half away.

OPPOSITE: The Pagoda on Mount Penn.

A lot of old local business vehicles can be found in the museum: electric trucks from the Curtis Publishing Company in Philadelphia and the Wilkinson Laundry in Reading (with a Himmelberger Wagon Works body also from Reading), and Ford mail trucks that were developed at the Boyertown Auto Body Works in 1949.

Nearby Reading was a really busy place early in the 1900s. When you hear "Fleetwood," you think Cadillac. But before GM acquired the company in 1927, it was producing custom cars in Fleetwood, Pennsylvania, right outside the city. In 1912 Sternberg was making a car that could travel at 60 miles an hour, also in Reading. The 1914 DILE automobile (Reading once again) was considered a competitor to Ford's Model T.

Those who are tired of looking at cars—or waiting for a companion to get his head out from under a hood—may like the license plates or artwork on display. In the days before customized license plates, people sometimes collected each plate by year. Usually they ended up nailed to a garage wall. The museum has a complete Pennsylvania blue-and-gold license set from 1907 to 1970, the days before personalized plates. And the "Gallery of the American Automobile" is a collection of color prints of automobiles by Clarence Hornung.

Looking for the right weekend to visit? Every Labor Day weekend, the museum holds the Duryea Day Antique and Classic Car Show, complete with contests such as "best antique car." Whenever you go, if you have time, drive up to Reading and see the Pagoda. It now has its own small museum. Just don't take Duryea Drive in high gear.

Christian Sanderson Museum

A sign outside the Christian Sanderson Museum reads: "If your tour does not include the Sanderson Museum, you are not being given the opportunity to see one of the area's real gems."

Let me go even further than that. If you visit only one museum described in this book, make it this one.

The Christian Sanderson Museum in Chadds Ford is truly an experience not to be missed. You've probably never even heard of Chris Sanderson (I feel free to call him Chris because in the course of an afternoon I came to know him well). He was born in 1882 and died in 1966—a significant span in world history. But Chris made no worldwide imprint. He was a schoolteacher, historian, fiddle player, and square-dance instructor. Probably his most public and lasting act as a historian was to help preserve the Brandywine Battlefield as a historic landmark.

Chris still managed to put himself squarely into history, though, simply by collecting. He acquired. He archived. He stockpiled bits of history in whatever house he was living in. And he didn't throw away *anything* he considered significant, which was *everything*.

The eight rooms of the Sanderson Museum—although wonderfully organized—may not appear to be a cohesive unit at first, but the visitor eventually gets the idea. The Sanderson family collected history—U.S., world, and their own. They made no distinction; it was all important to them. Hanna Carmack Sanderson, Chris's mother, shared with her son both a home and the family passion for collecting, until her death in 1944. Chris continued on, even saving the Christmas ornament his mother had hung on the tree the day before she died (still attached to the twig she hung it on).

A tulip poplar bloom, now preserved in a little plastic bag and meticulously labeled, was one of Chris's first acquisitions. His grandfather presented ten-year-old Chris with the bloom, cut from a tree planted by George Washington at Mount Vernon. I don't know where he got the piece of tile from Eva Braun's bathroom (she was Hitler's mistress) or the sand from the first atomic bomb blast (the July 1945 test in White Sands, New Mexico), but both are clearly marked and on display in the museum.

Some items are what we expect from a collector, such as autographs—Shirley Temple, Jefferson Davis, even Chiang Kai Shek—and Victorian valentines. Other pieces are seemingly insignificant. Who would think to pick up sawdust from a Billy Sunday revival meeting? Who would save the shoestrings he had worn to Harry S Truman's inauguration? (Chris didn't miss an inauguration from Teddy Roosevelt in 1905 to Lyndon Johnson in 1964.) And who would save their own dyed Easter eggs?

To amass a collection as large as Chris's took some assistance. His friends—and he had many—helped by acquiring

One of Chris's drawings.

things he wanted or they thought he might like. Veterans of the Civil War at the fiftieth anniversary of the Battle of Gettysburg gave him the purse that had been in the apron pocket of Jennie Wade (the only civilian killed at the Battle of Gettysburg). While some people may not see the significance of a simple leaf, Chris knew it came from the funeral wreath laid by President Woodrow Wilson on the grave of the Marquis de Lafayette.

Since he lived in the Chadds Ford area, it is no surprise that Chris was friends with the Wyeth family. They called him "Sandy" and all three—N. C., Andrew, and Jamie— painted his portrait. The museum honors their friendship by including pieces of Wyeth art. Although one room contains the majority of the Wyeth works, others are distributed throughout the house as they pertain to certain aspects of Chris's life. Andrew was so moved by the sight of Chris's mother in bed the day before she died that he went home and sketched her portrait.

Chris was also a prolific note writer and he saved his scribblings as he did everything else. When he died, the house contained over 4,000 handwritten notes. Some notes told visitors where they might find him ("at Andy Wyeth's") and some were reminders to himself, with instructions to "find . . ." (whatever it was he had misplaced).

Photographs in the museum illustrate the house as it was when Chris lived there. As you might expect for so vast a collection, the house was less than tidy. Chris could only sleep on one third of his bed because the rest was filled with a portion of his possessions.

Thomas Thompson, a friend of Chris's and the museum's

"CHRIS AT HIS DESK"

curator, has done a magnificent job of organizing and displaying this extensive collection. Walls are covered, cases are full, yet all are easy to view. Shortly after Chris's death, Thompson, a retired office manager, started cleaning and cataloging the items because, as he told me, Chris "didn't get

Christian Sanderson
Museum

Routes 1 and 100

Chadds Ford, PA 19317

(610) 388-6545

www.sandersonmuseum.org

HOURS:

Saturday and Sunday 1 P.M.–4:30
P.M., and by appointment.

DIRECTIONS:

From the Pennsylvania Turnpike,
take the Route 100/Downingtown
Exit. Go south on Route 100. The
Christian Sanderson Museum is
on Route 100, just a few buildings
north of Route 1. Parking is available at the Chadds Ford Inn (at
the intersection), and a walkway
at the back of that parking lot
leads to the museum.

the recognition he deserved." The museum, in Chris's last
home, is organized by subject, such as war, the Wyeths,
Chris's days as a schoolteacher. Tours are self-guided, so a
visitor can spend as much time absorbing each collection as
desired, but a guide will be provided if you ask for one.

Anyone born in the twentieth century should see this
museum. It's a history lesson, a nostalgia trip, a fascinating
look at one man's life. Everyone will recognize something.
My sister Candace and I were amazed when we realized that
we'd spent nearly two hours peering into cases and gazing at
wall displays. Unbelievably, only 2,000 people visit every
year. Go see this place and get to know Chris Sanderson.
You won't regret it.

The Insectarium

There's a reason they're called "bugs." Insects are probably one of the least popular branches of the animal kingdom. Creepy-crawlies. We think they have too many legs and too many places to hide. That they only exist to poison us. Nasty little thing, where's my shoe so I can kill it?

So if we only want to hasten these creatures' demise, why have an Insectarium? Because they fascinate us (especially when we're young). Because the insect realm is far larger than we ever see in Pennsylvania—so much more than mosquitos, spiders, and ticks. How often do we find iridescent butterflies or horned beetles? Or see a cocoon or honeybee hive up close?

When I learned about the Insectarium, it seemed ironic that it was operated by an exterminating company—the opposite of their reason for being. But, on reflection, what better place for a bug collection? My niece Annie (self-proclaimed arachnophobe) and I had to go inside the main office of Steve's Bug Off Exterminating to pay our museum admission. Only time in all my travels I've seen bug spray offered in a museum gift shop. They also provide brochures on bug problems, with titles like "The Facts of Lice." Nothing like exterminators with a sense of humor.

We walked up to the second floor and into the Insectarium. My jaw must have dropped when we walked in the first room. Thousands of mounted butterflies and moths, in cases, covered one half of the room. I've never seen so many. They came from the collection of Philadelphian William Boscoe, who inherited a significant butterfly and moth collection and since 1948 has added his own. Most are not identified, some are clearly duplicates. Some are mounted above a mirror so that you can see the reverse side as well. It's breathtaking to see such delicate beauty and exquisite grace up close. I wished they were alive so I could see them fly.

Pulling myself away from the butterflies, I looked to see what else the room offered. Child-size kiosks dot the room,

each side offering a multiple-choice quiz, with questions children might ask: "How many brothers and sisters?" "How long do insects live?" and "How fast do insects go?" While Annie and I pressed all the buttons, two little girls ran through the spacious room, laughing and chasing each other while wearing butterfly wings (later, a little boy had on a pair and his parents called them "bee wings").

The other wall contained beetles—big fat ones—also in cases. Tropical beetles and horned beetles. More beetles than I knew existed in the world. But it didn't make me not want to hear those hard shells crunch as I mentally stepped on them. We also saw the first live exhibits in the museum: a case of honeybees, and a case of termites. The latter was really my first and only "ick" in the place.

More surprises than we knew awaited us when we climbed to the museum's upper floor, the building's third floor. Terrariums line the walls, each with a different living creature, mostly scorpions or spiders. Annie announced that she likes scorpions. I was horrified. Doesn't she know that scorpions climb in a sleeping bag in every single desert movie? Cowboys are never safe from the deadly scorpion!

But there she was, face up against the glass, admiring the desert hairy scorpion, the tailless whip scorpion, even the emperor scorpion, which is the *largest* but not the *deadliest* scorpion (this makes no difference to me). Despite their glass cases, Annie stayed a little further away from the horned baboon tarantula, the black widow spider, and the rabid wolf spider.

As we were wandering around, we ran into museum education supervisor Jeanette A'psis, who transformed our already fascinating visit into a hands-on presentation. Jeanette pulled up a few seats for us near some tanks containing a whip scorpion, a Honduran curly tarantula, a chocolate-colored millipede, and a Madagascar hissing cockroach. Then, to my surprise, she very gently lifted the tarantula out of its tank and introduced us to Hairyette. This hairy little creature with a little bald spot on her lower back didn't look like anything in a horror movie. Jeanette explained how Hairyette defends herself; her back legs help her throw hairs, "which will give a good rash." She encouraged us to pet the spider, which we did—reluctantly, but we did. Hairyette was soft, almost like a kitten with really short hair.

So much for Annie's arachnophobia. After that we met and petted Vinny the whip scorpion. He puts acid on his tail and whips it around to blind his enemies. We also got up close and personal with Hershey the chocolate millipede. Annie loved the death-feigning beetle, which Jeanette had trouble convincing it was in danger so that it would indeed feign death.

I noticed a crowd forming as Jeanette talked to us. Two children came and sat right up front. Their parents stood behind us. We were all spellbound as she talked about spiders and snakes and warned us that bright colors mean danger: remember, "Red next to yella, kill a fella; black, that's a friend of Jack."

After working at the Philadelphia Zoo, Jeanette came to the Insectarium five years ago. Now she takes traveling exhibits to schools and works to educate people about the creatures she works with every day. Some weekends are reserved for special events, like A Bug's Meal (in November) and the Bugs of Old Ireland (March). Jeanette blames Hollywood for our fear of tarantulas and scorpions. Guess she's never known any cowboys.

While Jeanette was talking, I noticed a child yelling just outside the room, "I don't wanna eat a bug, I don't wanna eat a bug!" His parents finally convinced him that he didn't have to eat any bugs and this sniffling three-year-old in bee wings joined us. No one knew how he got that idea. Jeanette informed us we were a few weeks early for the edible insect weekend (don't think I was sorry).

This is a great place for both grownups and kids. But you don't have to eat a bug and you don't have to pet a spider—unless you want to.

The Insectarium

8046 Frankford Avenue
Philadelphia, PA 19136
(215) 338-3000
www.insectarium.com

HOURS:

Monday–Saturday 10 A.M.–4 P.M.

DIRECTIONS:

Follow I-95 North to the Cottman Avenue Exit. Follow Cottman Avenue (Route 73) until you come to Frankford Avenue. Make a right onto Frankford Avenue to 8046 Frankford Avenue. The Insectarium is the left between Rhawn Street and Welsh Road.

Lost Highways Archive and Research Library

"Archive and Research Library." Maybe that label sounds a little foreboding. But there are no "shush"-ing librarians here. If I were to name this place, I might call it "Things You've Only Seen in Old Postcards or Road Movies." Maybe you can find another name for it. Whatever you call it, this museum dedicated to the idea of the American road is certainly freewheeling.

Lost Highways has been around for ten years but it took more than reading a map for me to find it. Could that be what makes it "Lost"? Maybe. As for "Highways," it's right in the middle of Philadelphia's historic district. Ben Franklin's house is a jaywalker's step away. Not exactly the Schuylkill Expressway. But Lost Highways is not about finding one's way or limited access traffic. It's about the road and an era that no longer exists—before McDonald's—when people had to pack picnic lunches, complete with a thermos of lemonade for any extended trips, when gas stations weren't found every ten miles and Breezewood's life as the Town of Motels was just somebody's dream.

The signs for Lost Highways are on the second floor of the

building (easily visible from across the street) and in the doorway. I rang the bell as my sister Candace peered in the shop windows on the street. When the door was opened, we walked up the old wooden stairs, unsure of what lay ahead.

When we reached the top of the stairs, we paused and looked around. To the left was a large open room with display cases. Colorful posters on the walls advertised the current two museum displays: "RV Roots: The Auto Camping Craze of the 'Teens and 'Twenties" and "The Family Car on Mars: The American Station Wagon, 1956–1962." "Mars?!" I said to my sister.

Then we turned to the right of the museum area and saw the large silver back-end of a Trailmobile trailer, which serves as a room divider. Behind the Trailmobile it's definitely twenty-first century, with all modern office equipment, computers, and light tables. This is the archive and library.

Todd Kimmell, who created Lost Highways with his wife Kristin, came out from behind the Trailmobile to greet us. He showed us the museum section, which is divided into two parts. Todd says one side—now the "RV Roots" display—will always be "dedicated to living on wheels."

On that side, I saw a dark brown piece of canvas and figured it was covering something up. It turned out to be a tent like nothing North Face has ever manufactured, I'll bet. In its lifetime, this three-sided tent would have been set up with the traveler's car as the fourth wall (now a cardboard car holds it up). I peered inside and saw a cot, a Kamp Kook-stove, dinner plates, a suitcase, three very similar jugs in a carrier, and two folding chairs. Kwite komfy! Todd explained that the three small jugs contained oil, gas, and water—

"The day of the PUSHBUTTON AUTOMOBILE is here."

—1950s car ad

everything a traveler with car trouble might need. (Well, maybe everything but a cell phone.)

Candace and I perused the display cases at our leisure. We saw postcards for traditional road destinations, like Yellowstone and the Cave of the Winds, as well as roads like the Lincoln Highway in Omaha. Picnic coolers, hood ornaments, the bylaws for the Motor Camping Association, a first-aid kit, thermoses, maps, travel booklets, and name plates for trailers and cars—pretty much anything road-themed that struck Todd's fancy. In the back, he has a very large motel sign for Flora's Court, which came from Kentucky.

Todd has his own diverse background. "I used to be a junk man for a living," he said. He was also a punk-rock DJ in Philadelphia clubs—b.k. (before kids), that is. Now he owns a graphics company. As with so many other small museum owners, the collecting bug bit him and didn't let go. He's still acquiring and has plenty more to put on display. Some of the posters hanging in the museum show something of Todd's vision of the past and future merged. Picture colorful old car advertisements with space-age themes in the background. I don't remember seeing Saturn (the planet, not the car) in that station wagon ad when I was a kid! For those who are really attracted to the idea of the "Family Car on Mars," his posters are for sale.

True to the building's age, and as of this writing, Lost Highways does not have air conditioning. So it would be best to visit some time other than an August afternoon. Todd hopes to add Saturday hours and someday possibly tour with the exhibit. But for now, Lost Highways is staying right where it is. You'll have no trouble finding it.

Lost Highways Archive and Research Library
307 Market Street, 2d floor
Philadelphia, PA 19103
(215) 925-2568
www.losthighways.org

HOURS:
Monday–Friday 9 A.M.–5 P.M. to tour the museum. Researchers should call for an appointment.

DIRECTIONS:
From I-676 (Vine Street), take the Eighth Street Exit. Go south on Eighth to Market Street. Turn left onto Market. Lost Highways is on the left side of Market Street, right before Second Street.

Moravian Pottery and Tile Works

This is potentially the most expensive museum you may visit. Not because of the admission fee, though. Looking at all those gorgeous handcrafted tiles is going to inspire you to redecorate: "Wouldn't this look good in the kitchen? . . . and the front hall needs to be redone . . . and, oh yes, that dull bathroom. . . ."

Henry Mercer founded the Moravian Pottery and Tile Works in 1898. Using Pennsylvania's abundant red clay, Mercer wanted to revive the art of tilemaking in Bucks County. At first try, his tiles were less than perfect, but once he began working with handcrafted tiles, he became a successful contributor to the thriving Arts and Crafts movement of the early 1900s. Mercer built the present structure in 1912 for his tile studio.

When Henry Mercer died in 1930, the tilemaking ended. In an effort to preserve this part of local history, officials there opened the museum in 1969; it is now run by the county's Department of Parks and Recreation. The art of tilemaking was revived at the Tile Works in 1974, with a goal to stay close as possible to Mercer's original methods. The only difference today is the use of electric kilns. The clay still comes from nearby Green Lane.

You may already be familiar with the Mercer Museum, which houses Henry Mercer's vast personal collection of preindustrial tools. In the late 1800s, Mercer realized that these tools were quickly disappearing in the sweep of the Industrial Revolution and decided to preserve that part of humanity's history. Both the Moravian and Mercer museums, as well as Fonthill, Mercer's home, are made entirely of hand-mixed concrete. On the same land, the house and the industrial museum are also open for tours. I chose the Moravian Pottery and Tile Works for this trip.

It was a cool, gray day when my friend Caitlin and I arrived at the Mercer estate. The color of the sky made the massive Spanish-mission–style building known as the Moravian Pottery and Tile Works seem foreboding and the grounds were quiet and empty. We didn't see a soul from the parking lot to the front door.

So it was a bit of a shock to walk inside. If it hadn't been for the low ceilings and the concrete walls, I would have thought I was in Home Depot. The gift shop was full of do-it-yourselfers, standing in front of rows of tiles for sale, asking each other, "Do you think this would look good on that wall?" and "I want to redo the floor, but I don't know quite what I want." Everyone was working on home projects.

Museum tours are scheduled for every half hour; we had about fifteen minutes to wait. We browsed through the tiles in the shop, came up with a few for ourselves, and watched some buyers laying out a tile pattern on a large table. We

found tiles on varied subjects: everything from bears to wild-cats, the signs of the zodiac, famous ships such as the *Bounty* and the *Santa Maria*, and the Four Gospels. It was hard to decide what to buy. I really did start thinking about a nice splashguard in my kitchen.

Before I could figure out how to explain a large tile purchase to my husband at home, though, our tour guide called us into the room that was Mercer's studio. This chilly, high-ceilinged chamber has a fireplace that couldn't keep the room warm, but the tiles on the walls make it seem less like a dungeon. We sat down for an informative seventeen-minute video on the history of the Pottery and Tile Works, how tiles are made and colored, and how Mercer came up with his designs.

When the video was over, the guide directed us up the castle-like, concrete stairs to the second floor. Here we were left on our own to wander through the tilemaking areas. We walked past the old brick kilns and slab rooms. We looked into the clay pit and found a bit of poetry: on the ceiling above the pit is written, "Keep me damp by the light of the lamp." Less lyrically, it would read "don't let the clay dry out."

Everything is well labeled so we had no difficulty understanding the tilemaking process. Since this is obviously a working museum, all along the tour route we saw clay. Big blocks of clay. Clay that had already been pressed into the shape of a tile. Rows of clay birds lying on pallets, no doubt waiting for glazing and the kiln. And freshly glazed pieces.

I always learn something in my museum visits, but sometimes it's not knowledge gained, it's more a lesson. This time it was "Don't ask stupid questions." Caitlin and I walked by a young man working with a large block of clay. I asked him, "What are you making?" He turned the clay over and, without looking up at me, said, "Tiles." Not much of a conversationalist, I surmised. Bird molds lay next to him, so I suspect that cube of clay was destined to become those beautiful birds. Next time I think I'll just watch and wait.

With the word "Moravian" in the name, I thought that the museum was somehow connected to the Moravian religious sect, like the Moravian Archives Museum in Lititz. But Mercer chose the word solely because his early tile patterns were from eighteenth-century cast-iron stoveplates. The Yucatan designs of Mayan sacrifice rituals made today are a far cry from those German stoveplates.

Mercer's tiles can be found outside Bucks County, at the John D. Rockefeller estate in New York, the Gardner Museum in Boston, and the National Press Club in Washington, D.C., to name a few of the more famous places. Closer to home, the floor of the Pennsylvania State Capitol in Harrisburg is covered in four hundred Mercer tiles commemorating Pennsylvania's history; it makes a good secondary tour.

The museum exists to illustrate the art of tile making. I did feel an urge to try it myself, but Play-Doh is really more my speed. But for those who find that clay is in their blood, the Tile Works offers ceramist apprenticeships and tile workshops.

We finished the tour at our own speed and walked back out into the gray day, a few tiles weighing down our bags. As we headed for home, we passed Fonthill, Mercer's home, which Mercer himself called "a museum of decorative tiles and prints." No doubt that will be my next visit.

Moravian Pottery and Tile Works

130 Swamp Road, Route 313
Doylestown, PA 18901
(215) 345-6722
www.buckscounty.org/departments/tileworks/

HOURS:

Daily 10 A.M.–4:45 P.M.

DIRECTIONS:

From the Pennsylvania Turnpike, take the Horsham/Willow Grove Exit. Go north on Route 611 and turn right onto Route 313 East. The museum is between North and Court streets. (Please note that those streets are labeled Court and North only on the right side of the street.)

Mummers Museum

The Mummers are as much Philadelphia as Mardi Gras is New Orleans. While outfits, skits, and the parade route may change over the years, one thing never does: if the weather's good (no snow, rain, or high winds—cold doesn't matter), the Mummers will don their feathers and sequins and strut on New Year's Day.

Maybe you've heard of the Mummers but never quite knew what they do. Philadelphia's Mummers Parade is a cross between a Las Vegas show and the best wedding you've ever attended. No ho-hum, smiling-and-waving beauty queens perched on flowered-covered floats. The Mummers Parade is wenches and clowns, music and dancing (Mummers don't march, they strut!), skits and improv, color and noise and revelry.

The Mummers tradition began in the 1700s when immigrants living in South Philadelphia performed for their neighbors on New Year's Day. It didn't become an organized event until the city asked the Mummers to help celebrate the completion of the new city hall. The Mummers weren't inclined to take their tradition out of the neighborhood until they heard that $1,700 in prize money was available. Their tune changed (probably to "Oh, Dem Golden Slippers," the most famous of Mummers tunes), and the Mummers held their first official parade down Broad Street in 1901.

Gone are the days of family members spending long hours making the costumes themselves or corralling volunteers to help prepare a routine. As they always have, the Mummers clubs (close to fifty of them)—either string band, fancy, fancy brigade, and comic—choose a theme. But now they pay "suit" (that's what the costumes are called) designers and makers, choreographers and truck drivers. Mummery is big business.

The "Going Up Broad Street" exhibit.

With all those professionals, expenses can run very high. A club can spend as much as $75,000 to $100,000 a year to get ready for their New Year's performance. In return, they are judged and awarded monetary prizes in many categories for their outfits, skits, and music. In 2002, 15,000 Mummers participated and $395,000 in prize money was awarded. (It sounds like a lot until you split it between all the divisions in all those clubs.)

On New Year's Day, the fancy brigades perform indoors at the Convention Center; they use a lot of props, maybe do

a skit, and wear more than one type of costume. The string band, fancy, and comic clubs follow the street parade route, entertaining with music, dance, and routines. Their path has changed many times over the years (but it always includes "Two Street"), and it's still changing, as they try to catch the best crowds, the best light, the best viewing areas.

When I began watching them in the mid-1960s, I knew I could never be a Mummer. They were reportedly all working-class men from South Philadelphia and liquor played a large role in their performances (well, it *was* cold). But that's not the face the Mummers wear today. Professionals join with blue-collar workers both behind the scenes and on the parade route. And women have been marching since (at least) the 1970s. And they're always looking for more volunteers—you really don't have to have been born with a cheesesteak in one hand and a Tastykake in the other to be a Mummer.

Call me unrealistic, but I was disappointed that the museum

exterior—multicolored though it is—isn't sequins. No feathers either. The first floor has a small "Winners' Circle" display of award-winning suits, next to a television where a parade video plays constantly. When I walked in the door, I saw a retired couple sitting in front of the video. When I left over an hour later, they were still there, watching the same video loop. I stopped to ask them if they had ever seen the parade live. These New Yorkers said they hadn't yet made it but vowed they wouldn't miss the next one. I guess mummery can be contagious.

The museum's main display, on the second floor, begins with a room full of suits. It's a treat to be able to see the construction and handiwork of each one up close. Some are recognizable articles of clothing, like pants and vests, studded with sequins and feathers (for one club alone, six to ten glue guns give their lives every year). Others are as much glamour as a marvel of engineering, such as the massive, six-sided "frame suits" worn by club captains. Back pieces (that large backdrop rising behind a marcher that can make a strong wind so dangerous) can weigh as much as 150 pounds. Imagine carrying that for an entire day!

Interactive displays show different aspects of the Mummers. You can hear what "Oh, Dem Golden Slippers" sounds like on a number of instruments just by pushing a button. A lighted map shows the changes in the parade route (the map is now scheduled to be revised once again). Flip cards show the Mummers from many years ago. And small suits are provided so that kids can try on Mummer outfits.

Museum curator Jack Cohen explained to me what it takes to get the parade off the ground—the scheduling, the

Mummers Museum

1100 S. Second Street
Philadelphia, PA 19147
(215) 336-3050
www.mummers.com

HOURS:

Tuesday–Saturday 9:30 A.M.–
5 P.M., Sunday 12 P.M.–5 P.M.

DIRECTIONS:

From I-76, the Schuylkill Express-
way, take I-676 East to the Eighth
Street/Chinatown Exit. Turn right
onto Eighth Street. Follow Eighth
Street to Bainbridge (first street
after South Street). Turn left on
Bainbridge and right on Second
Street.

maneuvering, the occasional last-minute recruitment when a
space needs to be filled. Cohen, a Northeast Philadelphia
native, works for the Department of the Treasury during the
week but volunteers at the museum every Saturday. He also
participates in the parade, as do his two daughters. By the
time we finished talking, I was ready to sign up, but that two-
hour commute would be a killer.

The museum's lower floor contains a social hall, which
they rent out for weddings or other events. Mummers coats
of arms and plaques adorn the walls. Tour groups coming
through are served lunch and entertained by the museum's
house band, The Hardly Ables. Since I was solo, I couldn't
get the package deal.

Despite what you might think, after New Year's Day the
Mummers do not just pack up their feathers and steal away
for another year. They continue to perform for each other
and for the public. On the Saturday after New Year's, parade
winners are serenaded by the rest of the Mummers. In addition to playing all over the city, clubs travel, too. I once saw
the Polish American String Band on the boardwalk in Wild-
wood, New Jersey, in the dead of summer.

So if you can't catch them New Year's Day, there are
many other—some much warmer—opportunities. But the
museum is open all year!

Museum of Mourning Art

What better place for mourning art than a cemetery? In the midst of Arlington Cemetery in Drexel Hill sits the Museum of Mourning Art, an elegant little museum dedicated to death and dying, mainly as viewed in the seventeenth and eighteenth centuries.

Unofficially, the tour begins outside. When we pulled into the cemetery entrance, I told my sister Candace to "look for Mount Vernon" because that's what I was told I'd find. It wasn't hard to spot. The building housing the museum, cemetery offices, and funeral home is an exact replica of George Washington's Mount Vernon, without the wings.

Candace accompanied me because she likes Victoriana; we did not know the time frame featured when we arrived. We expected hair jewelry, some celluloid memorials, perhaps a piece of needlework. But the museum concentrates on earlier times and we saw a lot that was unfamiliar to us.

Our tour guide, Regina Hunter, met us in the lobby. Before we entered the museum, she showed us around the rest of the building. All the modern conveniences are present, of course, but the historical detail is impressive. Aside

from essential office furniture, the interior is decorated completely in the Federal period, from the molding around the ceiling right down to the pattern on the carpet. The drapes are from the governor's palace in Williamsburg. Even the flowers that decorate the rooms are heirloom varieties that would have been grown during Federal times.

From the outer lobby we walked into the cemetery chapel, inspired by Bruton Parish Church in Williamsburg. The chapel pews are 150 years old, the floorboards 200 years old. It is a beautiful place, bright and sunny, and much warmer than I would have expected in such a setting. Weddings have even been held in that chapel.

We then walked over to the museum, through a side door off the lobby. The museum is dimly lit to protect the art from light damage. Taking photos is not allowed. Cases safeguard some works, others are hung on the wall. We found much printed material, such as engravings and books, featuring the stages of life, the hour of death, tombstones, and the afterlife. Emblem books gave moral messages about life and death in words and pictures. Not exactly light reading. I found the lantern clock, circa 1660, interesting. Ringing loudly, it alerted the family to tragic events. The clock hands were stopped to mark the owner's hour of death.

Some customs have changed significantly in the last three hundred years. We no longer consider it proper to have picnics in cemeteries, but it was common as late as the 1800s. Black is no longer the only color worn to funerals. The museum's display of funeral and mourning clothes shows outfits for men, women, and children. If the deceased had an adequate estate, that money might have been used to pay for those clothes. Major cities even had stores that specialized in funeral clothes.

Other parts of a funeral haven't changed at all. The number of people attending a funeral has always been a gauge of a person's popularity, but we no longer hire mourners. I wasn't aware that instead of reading a funeral notice in the newspaper and assuming the public was welcome, people used to receive invitations to a funeral. Obituaries and funeral invitations are part of the museum display.

One of the most memorable pieces in the museum is the cemetery gun, which was used to prevent grave robbing in the days before video cameras. Potential thieves entered the cemetery at risk of being shot if they weren't careful where they stepped. The guns were rigged to go off if they were disturbed. Unfortunately, the guns didn't distinguish thief from mourner, so they were eventually outlawed.

Today's fascination with celebrity death is nothing new. George Washington's passing brought the first outpouring of collective American grief. Many memorials were prepared in

Museum of Mourning Art

2900 State Road
Drexel Hill, PA 19026
(610) 259-5800

HOURS:
Tours by appointment only.

DIRECTIONS:
Take I-95 or I-75 to I-476, the
Blue Route. Get off at State Road.
Turn left at the bottom of the
ramp and follow State Road to
the cemetery.

paint, needlework, or sculpture. The museum displays some of those prints, either originals or reproductions. They also have a ring containing strands of Washington's hair, gifted by him to one of his relatives.

Although the museum is nothing if not dignified, there were still a few creepy parts. They have a bell on display from the days before embalming, when it might not have been that rare to accidentally bury someone alive. Just in case, a string was placed next to the body in the casket, with a bell above ground, so that if a mistake had been made and the person was still alive, he/she could ring the bell. Of course, the bell ringer would have to hope someone was having a picnic or just hanging around the cemetery.

If you haven't had enough of the historical, walk or drive back behind Mount Vernon to the mausoleum, a replica of Thomas Jefferson's Monticello. And the cemetery gardens, designed by James Buckler, landscape architect from the Smithsonian, are modeled after Jefferson's gardens at Monticello. Like I said, they didn't miss a single detail.

This is not a place for active children. They wouldn't find much to interest them after the cemetery gun. But it is an extraordinary place to learn about how people looked at death hundreds of years ago.

Richard Allen Museum

Maybe you think you know Philadelphia. You think you've been to every historical marker in Olde City and surrounding areas. You've followed the path from the Liberty Bell to Ben Franklin's first post office to the Betsy Ross House. But have you stopped at the Richard Allen Museum? Do you even know where it is?

Among blocks of pretty brick rowhomes, the Mother Bethel A.M.E. Church stands proudly at the corner of Sixth and Lombard Streets. Inside is a small museum dedicated to one of the most influential American men of the late 1700s and early 1800s. Richard Allen (1760–1831) was born into slavery but before his life was over he would buy his freedom, become a minister, and establish the first African Methodist Episcopal Church, a congregation that now counts more than 2.5 million members.

I read about Richard Allen before I scheduled my tour (see www.ushistory.org/tour/tour_bethel.htm). Sometimes it's hard to absorb everything historical in one museum and I wanted some background on Allen before my visit. Then one morning I entered the side door of the grand old church

Richard Allen built this pulpit for his own use.

and the secretary introduced me to my guide, Mrs. Katharine Dockens.

Although this is a small museum, the focus is not restricted to one narrow subject. Mrs. Dockens and I covered religion, Philadelphia, the Revolutionary War, early U.S. government, and abolition because they were all part of Richard Allen's life.

By the time he was twenty-one, Richard Allen was a free man. During the Revolutionary War he was a Teamster, carrying supplies to the troops. He also began preaching and by 1786 he was so well known that he was invited to preach at St. George's in Philadelphia, now the world's oldest Methodist church in continuous service.

As a direct result of Allen's preaching, St. George's black congregation grew. Allen asked permission to establish a black church to address their specific needs, but the Methodist elders would not agree. Allen and Absalom Jones then started the Free African Society, an organization to aid blacks who needed help, whether financial, medical, or spiritual.

But the new Society wasn't enough to satisfy Richard Allen. He felt the blacks of Philadelphia needed their own church. In 1791, with his own money, he purchased the land on which Mother Bethel Church now stands. Mrs. Dockens told me it has the distinction of being the only piece of land in the United States continually owned by African Americans since colonial times. But there were disagreements among the future congregants about whether the denomination would be Episcopalian or Methodist. The St. Thomas African Episcopal Church—the first black church in Philadelphia—was eventually built at Fifth and Walnut Streets.

Never idle but still without his own church, Allen continued to preach and help others. He also ran his own shoe-making business. During the yellow fever epidemic of 1793, he helped doctors and families despite the health risks. During the War of 1812 Allen and Jones would organize a black militia to defend Philadelphia from British invasion.

Finally, he was granted permission by the Methodists to build his own church, which would become Mother Bethel. Over time there would be four successive buildings. The first was a former blacksmith shop, moved from Walnut Street to Sixth and Lombard. Next, the "Roughcast Church" was built in 1804 and dedicated in 1805. The Red Brick Church was built in 1841. The church standing today was started in 1889 and dedicated in 1890.

When Mrs. Dockens and I walked downstairs to the museum she first showed me a wall mural by James Dupree. It portrays some of the events in Richard Allen's life, among them the Four Mother Bethels; the second Black Masonic Lodge, which was started by Allen and Jones; and the yellow fever epidemic. It is a good overview of his life.

In a small tiled room near the mural sits the crypt of Richard Allen, who is entombed along with his wife Sarah and A.M.E. pastor Morris Brown. Allen's original grave-

Richard Allen Museum

Mother Bethel A.M.E. Church
419 S. Sixth Street
Philadelphia, PA 19147
(215) 925-0616

HOURS:
Tuesday–Saturday 10 A.M.–3 P.M.
by appointment.

DIRECTIONS:
From I-676 take the Eighth Street Exit. Turn left on Race and right on Sixth Street. Mother Bethel Church is at Sixth and Lombard.

stone, laid on top, lists his accomplishments—as you might expect, it is a lengthy tribute.

Like many people, I prefer to see real pieces of a person's life; it brings the historical figures closer. Plates, platters, and bowls from the Allen household are on display. Some of the pews from the blacksmith shop/church still exist. These benches could be used as tables, too, since the church doubled as a school. The true monument to his career as preacher, beyond the existence of the church, of course, is Allen's pulpit, which he built, and his prayer stools and chair. All show wear from his use.

Church history is not forgotten either. The Hall of Bishops shows drawings or photographs of every A.M.E. bishop to the present day. Other photographs document historical moments: the paying off of the church mortgage in 1949, the A.M.E. bishops in front of the Justice Department in Washington, D.C., for the *Brown v. Board of Education* ruling in 1954, and the first woman elder in the church.

The end of the museum tour includes a visit to the church upstairs. While she showed me the beautiful woodwork and stained glass, Mrs. Dockens let me know why she is so knowledgeable about Richard Allen. She said quietly, "Richard and Sarah are my great-great-grandparents." I felt as though I was as close to history as I would ever get.

The much better-known Afro-American Museum is just a few blocks away from Mother Bethel. All over the state are sites with a connection to the Underground Railroad, including the African-American Museum in Reading with its dramatic hiding place for slaves. But there is no denying that this is the place to start. This is the cradle of liberty.

The Shoe Museum

Shoes have always been somewhat of an affliction to me. From my childhood days shod in plain brown orthopedic shoes (even black and white saddle shoes were a treat!) to finding as an adult that nearly every other woman who wears my size has been to the store before me, it has not been an easy life for my feet. I hesitated about going to the Shoe Museum, but I thought that maybe I'd find the answer to a better shoe.

So—with this attitude—is it wiser to go alone or to take along a smaller-footed friend who thinks that no trip to Nordstrom's is complete without a run through the shoe department? I chose the latter and took Caitlin. She knows shoes.

We arrived for our appointment—it's required for admittance—and were greeted by curator Barbara Williams. A quick elevator ride to the sixth floor and we stepped into a hallway lined with glass cases. This is not Payless with walls of shoes in boxes. Each museum shoe—over 100 on display at any time—is carefully preserved under glass. More than 800 more pairs are in storage, waiting for their moment in the footlights.

LEFT TO RIGHT: Ocelot oxfords, 1920s. Women's "yaller" boots, circa 1910. Chinese lotus shoe. Moroccan sultan's shoe. Joe Frazier's boxing shoes.

The Shoe Museum is part of the Temple University School of Podiatric Medicine's Center for the History of Foot Care and Footwear. Like the Mummers Museum, the Shoe Museum was started in the bicentennial year because the city wanted tourists to have places to visit. The collection has grown so much over the years that it's squeezed like Cinderella's stepsister in the glass slipper.

Barbara showed us around and explained the different shoes. Although she said she's "no fashion expert," she's very knowledgeable about shoes and their history. Caitlin's expertise came in handy when Barbara started talking about the BATA Museum in Toronto—it seems this is the Mecca of shoe worshippers. According to Barbara, "The BATA has everything." Caitlin nodded. What could I say?

Want to get closer to a celebrity's feet? Do Robert Mitchum's cowboy boots or Sally Struthers's blue satin platforms from her days on *All in the Family* interest you? Sports figures are big at the Shoe Museum, as you might imagine.

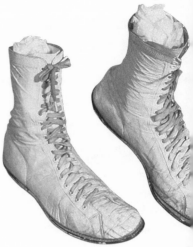

Billie Jean King, Arnold Palmer, Joe Frasier, André Agassi, and Dr. J. Even Bernie Parent's skates.

Not just a bit of fluff like maribou slippers, this museum has substance. Remember, "Shoe is not just a length and a width." We all know shoes have heels and soles and (sometimes) tongues. But what is a "shoe last"? It doesn't mean how long a shoe remains in good shape. A shoe last is the piece of wood or plastic around which a shoe is molded. A good last will mean a good fit.

Who knew there were so many types of shoes in the world? We saw Egyptian burial sandals, Victorian bridal footwear, children's shoes, South African clogs, Eskimo boots, iron diving boots, ballerina shoes, a size 18 shoe, Earth shoes, clogs for clogging, and really *really* high-heeled shoes. I was surprised to find out that there are so many different types of footwear. I was not surprised, however, to learn that women have four times as many foot problems as men. "Fashionable" and "comfortable" never appear side by side, do they?

The Shoe Museum

Eighth and Race Streets
Philadelphia, PA 19107
(215) 625-5243
podiatry.temple.edu/museum/
museum.htm

HOURS:

Wednesday and Friday mornings
only. Appointment required.

DIRECTIONS:

From I-676 (Vine Street), take the
Eighth Street exit. Go south on
Eighth. The museum is on the
sixth floor of the Temple University School of Podiatric Medicine,
the large white building on the
corner of Eighth and Race.

RIGHT: Evening shoe with six-inch heel,
1890s.

What made the most enduring impression on me were the tiny shoes worn by Chinese women whose feet had been bound. The practice involved wrapping cloth around a baby girl's feet to stunt their growth until she was five or so. Her feet ended up about half the size of normal adult feet and many, many females were crippled by the practice.

I appreciate a good shoe even more since my museum visit, but by the end of the tour even well-shod Caitlin was glassy-eyed. Pennsylvania is fortunate to have the best shoe museum in the United States; go to the BATA in Toronto if you want anything better. Parts of it are not for the faint of heart—my feet still hurt at the thought of binding—but if you enjoy shoes, this is the museum for you!

Wharton Esherick Museum

When my husband, Joe, and I (along with some friends) arrived at the Wharton Esherick Museum, the rest of our tour group was standing in the driveway waiting for us. We were late. The Esherick is not easy to find if you're not a local. But if you are, just wind your way through Valley Forge Park from Phoenixville toward Paoli and turn up the hill at the little round stone house.

When Wharton Esherick decided to build his art studio on the hill behind the home he shared with his wife and daughters in the mid-1920s, he applied the same ideas he put into his artwork. Esherick hated straight lines, so the building—outside and in—is full of curves, right up to the roofline.

The tour began in the driveway, looking down at the studio. Our guide, Esherick's daughter Ruth Bascom, pointed out the unique touches to the wood and concrete edifice, including the copper seaming on the roof, the dovetailed corners (on a building!), and the autumn leaves painted on the studio's silo. No wonder Esherick's studio, which took forty years to build, is now a National Historic Landmark for Architecture.

Spiral stairs Esherick built from his studio to his apartment above.

As another person whose name I did not recognize, I was glad to learn about Wharton Esherick (1887–1970), known as the "dean of American craftsmen." Trained in painting, Esherick started carving wood in 1919, creating many beautiful sculptures over the years. Eventually, he turned to making furniture "out of necessity," says his daughter. After all, it paid the bills. But, she adds, he had always "considered himself a sculptor."

Esherick designed his studio with barn-size doors at ground level so that trucks could drop off large pieces of wood for his projects. That same delivery area is now a showcase for Esherick's sculptures. It's the only place on the tour that feels "art museum like."

Yet the entire studio is still not very "serious" (read "dull"). It was obvious to me throughout the tour that Esherick clearly had a sense of fun along with his vision. He once bought a large number of hammer handles at an auction, not sure what he was going to do with them. They became chairs. Wagon wheels became chairs as well. And even if he wasn't limited by material, he might have an idea out of the ordinary. A library ladder in the studio is narrow at the bottom and wide at the top.

Evidence of Esherick's style is everywhere. Even when making furniture he was first a sculptor. He shunned handles and right angles in

Wharton Esherick's studio.

chairs, desks, tables, and even lights. His tables and chairs have curves so graceful they persuade one to believe they were shaped by nature. And his artist eye was always aware of detail: even the studio's door latches are not squared.

Esherick was fortunate enough that, as he became more successful, he could hire assistants. He sometimes created a model for a piece of furniture and other workmen made the

"If you're not HAVING FUN doing what YOU'RE DOING, don't do it."

—Wharton Esherick

actual pieces. Although he had people to do his lathe work, the rubbing, and the carpentry, his daughter says, "His touch is in everything."

And our touch was in some places, too. As you would expect, we were discouraged from sitting on most of the furniture. But we were encouraged to touch some of the wood sculptures. If you've never thought of wood as "soft" or "warm," go to the Esherick. Silk, a baby's skin, a puppy's fur first come to mind. But they don't adequately describe the feel of that wood. "Seductive" definitely does. It is evident that Esherick loved wood and knew how to bring its beauty to new heights.

The staircase from the studio to the apartment above is a highlight (and a reason to avoid this tour if you have trouble walking up stairs). It's a wooden, cantilevered, spiral staircase, complete with a mastodon-tusk rail. We climbed that staircase—which to me looked like it wouldn't support one of us, let alone a full group—to the apartment above, another Esherick creation, built in 1940.

And again his touch is everywhere. In the kitchen, the counters are curved around two walls, the shelves above the counters follow the same lines. The sink is copper. Obviously a man with priorities, Esherick made his own martini stirrer and salad tongs. The coathooks are portraits of the people who helped build the place. The dining-room floor may be "scrap wood," but it's the prettiest scraps I've ever seen.

Esherick was unexpectedly practical in some ways. He added lights in his cabinets so that when a cupboard door is opened a light goes on; his desks have similar features. His bed, with a full set of drawers underneath, was raised to the level of the window so that he could lie in bed and have a fantastic view of the valley below while thinking about what to create.

When we finished viewing the kitchen and walked out on the deck, I knew the tour was over. But I was sorry to see it end because I knew there was more to Wharton Esherick than I had absorbed on that one trip. As we left I decided that I would be back before long for a second visit. And next time, I'll be punctual.

Wharton Esherick Museum

P.O. Box 595
Paoli, PA 19301-0595
(Horseshoe Trail, Valley Forge)
(610) 644-5822
www.levins.com/esherick.html

HOURS:
Weekdays 10 A.M.–4 P.M., Saturday 10 A.M.–5 P.M., Sunday 1 P.M.– 5 P.M. Tours by reservation only.

DIRECTIONS:
The museum recommends that you call for directions.

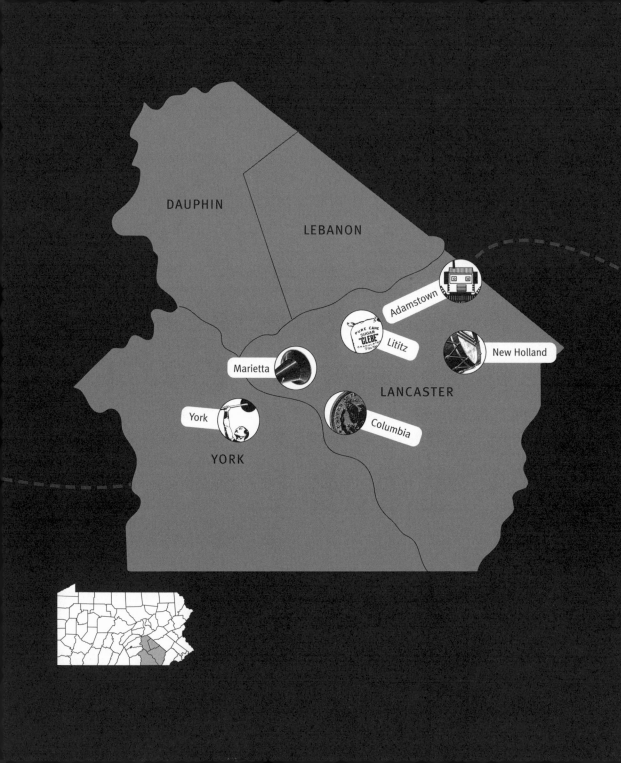

DAUPHIN

LEBANON

Adamstown

Lititz
PURE CANE SUGAR "GLEBE" GRANULATED 7 lbs Net

New Holland

Marietta

LANCASTER

York

Columbia

YORK

DEEP IN THE LOWER SUSQUEHANNA VALLEY

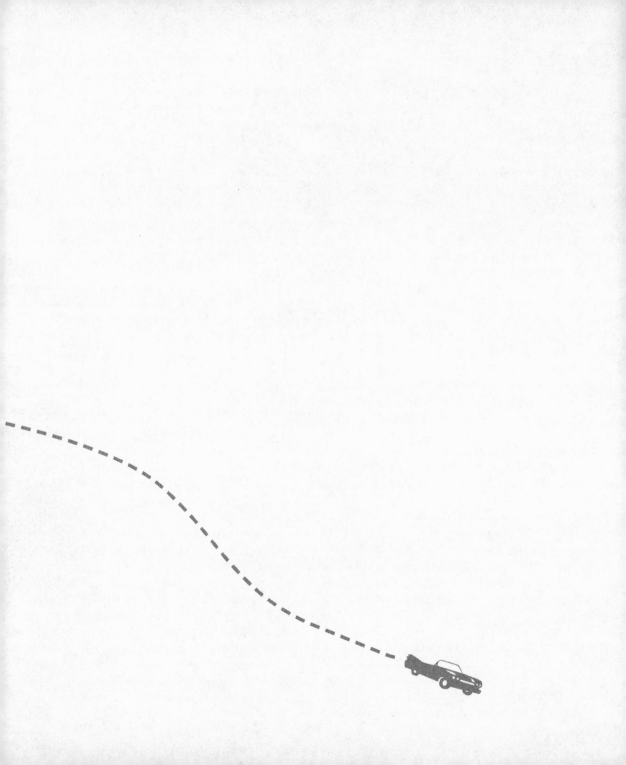

Bob Hoffman Weightlifting Hall of Fame and Museum

No one would confuse Muscle Beach, California, with York, Pennsylvania. But—minus the sand and the ocean—the annual gathering of bodybuilders at the York Barbell Strength Spectacular is nearly as enticing. I can now say I know people who think that being able to lift 250 pounds into the air, over their heads, is not only a good idea but something to strive for.

Once again out of my element, I decided to go with the flow (or, in this case, the clean and jerk). The Bob Hoffman Weightlifting Hall of Fame and Museum is owned by York Barbell, a well-known weight and exercise equipment manufacturing company. I was there for the Strongman Challenge on the final day of the weekend's festivities.

As I walked toward the museum building in the hot summer sun, I noticed four men standing in the shade, their enormous biceps bulging out of muscle t-shirts, their massive thighs in tight shorts—in other words, what you expect at a Strongman Challenge. And then two women, discussing a failed romantic relationship, passed me in the parking lot. I considered turning around and joining

Warming Up Exercise

DUMBELL EXERCISES

1. Dumb-bell Swing

5. Chest Deepening

2. Alternate Press

6. Alternate Curl to Shoulder Then Press Overhead

3. Forward and Lateral Raise With Straight Arms

7. Holding Dumb-bell Overhead Reach Down and Touch Toe

4. One Arm Press

1. Two Arm Curl

3. Deep Knee Bend on Toes

9. Rise on Toes

them—their conversation was more my speed—but I knew I had a job to do.

The name may be "Strong*man*" but this is an equal-opportunity competition. In the morning, women had pulled a sand-filled jeep up a hill; men did the same with a sand-filled van. I arrived in the early afternoon, just before the standing press competition (that means standing and lifting a large amount of weight over one's head in a clean motion). But I would have to wait a little while for that event and so I went inside.

I felt a little self-conscious as I entered in my flowered-print sundress and sandals; I thought I'd stick out as "Not One Who Exercises." But the museum was full of people, young and old, muscular and flabby, washboard abs and spare tires. Some were perusing the uncirculated issues of *Strength and Health* magazine sold in the lobby, others were signing up for competitions. I wisely resisted the temptation to test my own strength. Instead, I wandered among the exhibits, looking at dumbbells and strongman belts and statues of ideal physiques.

Bob Hoffman, the Father of World Weightlifting, pursued his passion. With the profits from his York oil-burner business, Hoffman promoted both international and Olympic weightlifting competition. The statue in front of the museum bears his likeness (at least from the neck up). You can learn of Hoffman's life story by way of the museum—and see some personal non-weightlifting-related artifacts such as his bear collection—but John Fair's *Muscletown USA: Bob Hoffman and the Manly Culture of York Barbell* gives a far more detailed picture of this colorful man's life and is worth the read.

Hoping I could meet someone who knew his way around the weight room, I found Doug Kline of Bloomsburg reading the names listed in the Weightlifters' Hall of Fame. He told me that some big names in the weightlifting world, such as Bill Kazmaier, have attended past Strength Spectaculars. A member of the American Drug-Free Powerlifting Association, Kline has competed but now just lifts for his own enjoyment, three times a week for one and one-half hours. He said it's "very intense." I believe him.

York Barbell Strength Spectacular, 2001.

I also talked to Barbara Stephens of Wrightsville. When I asked her why she was there, she said, "It's Father's Day and this is what he [motioning toward her husband] wanted to do. Both of my sons lift, as does my husband. I don't think I'll ever be one of them." I no longer felt alone.

My attention was soon drawn to a small crowd gathered in the center of the museum. I couldn't see the speaker, but I overheard him say, "I was eight or nine years old when I first saw him bite a spike in half. I couldn't believe it." The spike-biter was Joseph Greenstein, known as the Mighty Atom, "The Little Man with Tremendous Power," and one of the

Bob Hoffman Weightlifting Hall of Fame and Museum

P.O. Box 1707
York, PA 17405
(717) 767-6481
www.yorkbarbell.com

HOURS:

Monday–Friday 9 A.M.–4 P.M.,
Saturday 9 A.M.–3 P.M.

DIRECTIONS:

From I-83 North, take the
Emigsville Exit. From the light, go
straight 1/4 mile. Entrance to the
York Barbell and the museum is
on the left.

first celebrity "strongmen." Strongmen often appear in cartoons and old movies, but this was real life.

In my visit I learned that weightlifting is not only about strength or endurance. Many people lift weights today to prevent bone loss or lose weight. I ended my museum tour talking to a woman about ballroom dancing. She had taken up lifting weights just to improve her dancing.

And with that, I waltzed out the door onto the museum's front lawn. Entire families, complete with folding chairs and picnic coolers, were there to watch their loved ones compete. When a father was trying to lift 250 pounds, his four-year-old son cheered, "C'monnnnnnn Dad-dee!" Another, older boy—maybe eleven—had a more specific goal in mind for his father: "Dad, you can do thirteen! I know you can!" That's thirteen lifts of 250 pounds—now that's a devoted son.

It was painful to watch (keep in mind, in my house my husband carries the groceries), but I couldn't have been more impressed. I could feel each lift in my back, my knees, my arms, my neck. It hurt even more as I watched the two women in competition, one in the under 132-pound body-weight class, one in the over-132. They were the only two competitors and therefore each won her class. Now that's my kind of contest!

Weightlifters already know about this place; for many, it's a vacation destination. For the rest of us, it's an interesting afternoon spent among the muscular.

First National Bank Museum

The banks of today are ugly. There, I said it. The days when banking was a special occasion, when customers were slightly intimidated by grand edifices of marble and granite, highly polished wood and floors—when you felt like your money was worth something—are gone. Each little building put up now is built for "convenience," the same as any other, as identical—and about as attractive—as a fast-food place. And that's a pity.

The First National Bank Museum, though, was a *real* bank. Not some branch attached to some anonymous strip mall, this was the one and only. And it has survived because the Motter family felt it would be a shame to lose this bit of Columbia's history.

The building at the corner of Second and Locust, just east of the Susquehanna River, has been a home, a hotel, a tavern, a library, and a bank. Now it's both home and museum. When my friend Patty and I pulled the porcelain knob doorbell at the entrance, Nora Motter Stark, owner and tour guide, came to the door.

Nora's parents, Lloyd and Jean Motter, had restored the bank and opened the museum in 1967, advertising it as "the

first and oldest bank museum in the United States." When her parents passed away and her siblings weren't interested, Nora and her husband, Michael Stark, moved into the home on the second and third floors and took over guardianship of the bank. The museum reopened in 1997.

A little history on the bank: In 1852 brothers Solomon and Daniel Detwiler leased the front parlor of 170 Locust Street from homeowner Gerhardt Brandt to create the Detwiler Brothers Bank. With railroads, canals, and the river, Columbia thrived and the Detwiler Brothers Bank was a success. In 1864, the Detwiler bank was chartered and renamed the First National Bank, which in 1917 merged with the Columbia National Bank to become the First-Columbia National Bank, which then moved to a building down the street (now a Moose Lodge annex). Not quite the bank merger mania of today, is it?

The Detwiler family remained at Second and Locust. Solomon Detwiler's daughter Effie opened the Columbia Free Public Library in the old bank. After the library moved out in the mid-1950s, the Motters purchased the property.

For the tour, Nora led us behind a large wooden door from the hallway into another time—a time before drive-up windows and ATMs. Here there is none of the present-day harsh fluorescent lighting, no long countertop with barely a privacy panel between transactions. In what had originally been the living room to the house sits a large, dark walnut teller's cage—note that's singular, as in *one* teller—facing the front door. It looked familiar only from the movies; I could picture Butch and Sundance sticking a gun between the brass bars and "requesting" a "withdrawal."

Behind the teller's cage is the bank vault. In an adjoining room is the president's office. The entire bank—teller's cage, president's office, and vault—would fit into some people's living rooms twice over. Even the bank branches in grocery stores today are larger.

While economical with space, the Detwilers clearly had an appreciation for the finer things. The teller's cage is beautifully polished dark walnut wood, with elaborately carved drawer pulls and a sterling silver teller's nameplate. The president's office includes a marble corner sink and Solomon Detwiler's nameplate on the desk, also sterling. Even if they'd had Formica then, I don't think they'd have used it in the countertops.

A glass case is placed along the wall where someone might have paused to write a check before cashing it. The case now contains currency, including Detwiler Brothers fractional bank notes, accounting ledgers, receipts for goods, and other banking ephemera collected by the Motter family. The original bank charter hangs on the wall. By reading through all this material, one could very easily imagine what life was like in nineteenth-century Columbia.

This is not a hands-off museum. Nora let us play with the bank's original check canceler—a hammer with an X carved into it, specially designed for the First National Bank and the tree stump it was pounded into. She also let us feel the coin sorter, where the wood is worn smooth from many tellers' hands. She says everyone wants to touch where the money was kept.

I felt like we were going into a forbidden space when we entered the bank vault, original to the Detwilers' bank. I kept

Deep in the Lower Susquehanna Valley

thinking the door might fly shut at any time (too many sit-coms, I know), but there was really no danger of that. A seal states it was fire-tested in 1852, when it was installed. Now it contains only the bank's cash books. No money. Really.

If crime was a concern, the bank didn't let it show. The bank charter specifies that a burglar alarm could be installed, but with two stipulations. It had to consist only of a bell and a string leading upstairs to the bank president's home and couldn't cost more than seven dollars. Only once did some-one attempt to rob the bank; a bullet hole remains in a shut-ter as the only evidence from that heist.

Nora will talk about local history as well as that of the bank. One of my favorite Civil War stories has to do with the deliberate burning of the bridge between Wrightsville (on the other side of the Susquehanna) and Columbia right before the Battle of Gettysburg. Without the bridge, the Confederate army couldn't cross and move east toward Philadelphia. So they turned back, only to meet the Union troops at Gettysburg. A few pictures of the bridge are on dis-play. She'll tell you the whole story if you ask.

This is another nice little museum. Along Route 30, you'll see roadside ads for the National Watch and Clock Museum in Columbia. Stop there if it interests you; it's very well done. But make the trek a few more blocks and see the First National Bank Museum, too. It's a real credit to Columbia and the Motter family.

First National Bank Museum

170 Locust Street
Columbia, PA 17512
(717) 684-8864

HOURS:
Tuesday–Saturday 1 P.M.–4 P.M., and by appointment.

DIRECTIONS:
Take the Columbia Exit from Route 30. Turn right at the end of the ramp and left onto Route 441 (Third Street). Follow 441 into town and make a right onto Locust Street. The bank is one block down, on the far left corner.

Kready's Country Store Museum

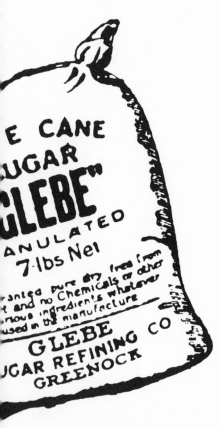

As a child, Lititz native Paul Brown had heard stories about Kready's General Merchandise store in neighboring Manheim. It was rumored that when E. E. Kready died in 1957, the family shut the store doors and left the place untouched, everything still on the shelves and walls.

As an adult, and an antiques dealer, Paul was intrigued by the legend. In 1993 he contacted Elias Kready Jr., the owner's son, who after much persuasion reluctantly let Paul see the store.

Indeed, the legend was true; the store appeared as it did in the 1950s. Paul immediately offered to buy the store's contents. After some finagling, Kready agreed to sell everything, but on his own terms. Paul could buy the entire inventory, piece by piece, as though he was a customer in the store, and only when Kready felt like selling. "At 2:30 in the afternoon," Paul told me with a smile. "If I was there at 2:29 or 2:31, he wouldn't sell."

His persistence paid off. Over the next three years, Paul gradually acquired every item in the store, as well as the building itself and all the outbuildings. Laundry soap, cereal

boxes, an entire dry goods department. Advertisements, seed catalogs, greeting cards. Holiday items, clothes, and medicines. Not just boxes, but the original contents of the boxes as well. The store had been open since the mid-1800s (under other owners) so items ranged in age as much as a century.

Certain sales are more memorable than others for Paul. When Kready sold him a Ken-L-Ration advertisement,

Paul commented that the dog's ears were ripped off. Kready said he had done it as a child. Paul told me, "He went back into the store, came out with the ears, and charged me one dollar apiece for them."

Once Paul took possession of the store, much work remained before his dream could be realized. In addition to the accumulation of nearly forty years of dust, the old store had been heated with a woodstove and soot lay over everything. Paul had to clean off each piece carefully. In some cases he shrink-wrapped items to preserve them.

In 1996, Paul opened Kready's Country Store Museum in the original Manheim building, before moving it in 1999 to its present location on Water Street in Lititz. While the present warehouse-sized building doesn't have the early twentieth-century appeal of the Manheim store, it has its own history. Originally, sound stages were constructed in the Water Street Studios, and national acts such as Kiss, Yes, and Kenny Rogers rehearsed there before tours.

No remnants of the sound studio remain. Paul removed the doors, flooring, and railing from the Manheim store and installed them at the Lititz location, so walking into the museum feels like walking into a real general store.

And what a store! Shelves are stacked and packed full of authentic household products, some local, some national. Strung above are advertisements—a half pound of cashews (43 cents) and Campbell's Soup (10 cents). The amount and condition of the items are exceptional. I must have stood still for ten minutes, just staring at one small section, trying to see everything. It took my breath away.

The store has more than just groceries. Popular culture,

Deep in the Lower Susquehanna Valley

circa 1935, in Shirley Temple memorabilia and Charley McCarthy and Mortimer Snerd. World War I propaganda materials: "Katch the Kaiser! Win the War!"

Someone spending an hour in the store would not nearly see the entire collection. Paul says he changes displays with the seasons and adds holiday items as appropriate. He also says he has "three full barns" of packaged food and sundries, and so rotates the stock.

The original sales agreement with Kready called for Paul to keep the collection intact and historically accurate, and to recognize the store's place in Lancaster County history. He has kept his promise. On the second floor of the museum, Paul has preserved furniture from the Kready home, such as a rattan baby carriage, and the "summer house" that sat behind the store in Manheim. He also displays a photo album of the renovations and early photos of the Kready family.

In these days of superstores and shopping malls, Kready's Country Store Museum unveils a part of American life that is gone forever. It really is a step—or two—back in time.

Kready's Country Store Museum

55 North Water Street
Lititz, PA 17543
(717) 626-5684

HOURS:
Monday–Friday 10 A.M.–5 P.M., Saturday 10 A.M.–4 P.M., and by appointment.

DIRECTIONS:
From Lancaster, go north on Route 501 to Lititz. Turn right onto Route 772 and go a few blocks to Water Street. Turn left. The museum is on the right.

Le Petit Museum of Musical Boxes

The first thing that comes to my mind when I think "music box" is pink, small, and plays an unidentifiable tune. When it's opened, a ballerina pops up. The collection at Le Petit Museum of Musical Boxes, though, has no ballerinas. Wooden boxes of all sizes, some with birds, cats, even the Baby Jesus—but no ballerinas. (I didn't miss them.)

One afternoon I drove to Marietta, a small picturesque town on the Susquehanna River. Many of the buildings are carefully decorated, their Victorian past preserved. On the main street, I passed homes painted purple and blue and green before coming to the brick Federal townhouse that is Le Petit Museum.

David Thompson, one of the owners, welcomed me warmly, asked where I was coming from, and then proceeded to give me a very melodious guided tour of the museum. Musical boxes have been a part of David's life since he was a child, when he kept a music box under his bed. As an adult, he began collecting them and, with partner George Haddad, opened the museum in 1997 so that other people could share in their enthusiasm.

The museum takes up the entire first floor of the town-house. Four rooms are wall to wall with musical boxes of all makes and themes. David was only too happy to wind up any box in which I expressed an interest. They didn't sound at all like I expected. No plink, plink, plink. The tone was rich, the music entertaining. I didn't always recognize the tune, but I knew it was quality.

You probably are familiar with cylinder music boxes. Wind one up and small strips of metal run over bumps on a rotating cylinder to make the song (I know I wasn't the only one to take that ballerina apart). But I wasn't aware that music boxes also came with round, flat disks. Same basic idea as the cylinder, but the metal plinks over holes instead of bumps. The Germans invented this exchangeable disk in 1886 so that they could hear more than one tune per box.

The biggest surprise for me this visit was realizing that, while this is a museum of musical boxes, it is also a museum on the history of musical engineering. The collection illustrates the progression of music box construction from a simple box to the nearly entertainment-center-sized Regina Orchestral, the largest music machine ever made in America. I learned that cylinder boxes are Swiss, and disk boxes can be German, Swiss, or American. The Regina Company, in business from 1893 to 1916, produced approximately 100,000 in all, with the Reginaphone one of the last combination music box/phonographs. Among them, a wide variety of music can be played, from popular tunes to marches and hymns.

Musical machines come in more than just the wooden box variety. I saw musical photo albums, dolls, birds, Christmas

Le Petit Museum of Musical Boxes

255 W. Market Street
Marietta, PA 17547
(717) 426-1154

$ 🛍

HOURS:

March–December: Saturday and Monday 10 A.M.–4 P.M., Sunday 12 P.M.–4 P.M.

RESTRICTIONS:

Two or more people required for tour, to maximum of eight.

DIRECTIONS:

Take the Route 441/Columbia exit from Route 30. Go 2 miles north on Route 441. Turn left at first traffic light (Route 23/Market Street). Follow East Market Street to 255 W. Market Street.

tree stands, even chairs that play music when you sit on them. I don't think of organs as musical boxes, but the museum's Diefenbacher organ, made in 1890, has a crank and therefore qualifies. The wax Baby Jesus, who reclines on a pillow on a box, lifts his head while his music plays. My favorite, though, was the French cat in a milk can. When it is wound, the cat pops up out of the can and licks its lips.

My guide was very knowledgeable about the boxes in the collection. When I asked him about where he acquired so many pieces, he told me that Lancaster County is a very good place to find musical boxes. He added, "Most of them don't have makers' names and you have to know what you're buying." Novice music box collectors, make a note of that.

The museum also has antique art glass, including some Tiffany. The dining room table is set for a formal dinner, adding to the beauty and charm of the room. At Christmas, the museum is thoroughly decorated in a Victorian style.

Although their creators made musical boxes as varied and detailed as possible, they couldn't keep up with the public's demand for music in the home. As David said to me, "The phonograph killed the music box." So it was not a happy ending for these little delights. But they live on in Marietta, playing for a small but interested audience.

The New Holland Band Museum

I am resisting an urge to break out in a rousing chorus of "Seventy-Six Trombones." This small museum in New Holland dedicated to the community band would be the pride of John Philip Sousa and the envy of Harold Hill. If you want rock 'n' roll, head west to Sharon and the Vocal Groups Hall of Fame and Museum. If you want "just band music"—trumpets and horns, woodwinds and drums—direct yourself to the New Holland Band Museum in Lancaster County.

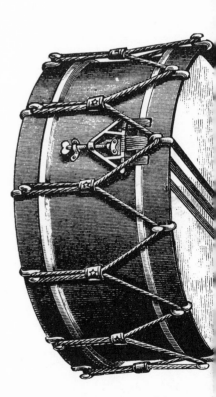

The community band is still a reality in many small towns in America. New Holland's own is called—of course—the New Holland Band. It was started in 1856 and is the oldest band in Lancaster County. Having gone through various incarnations and a number of names since its inception, including the Boys Band and the Victory Band (the latter in World War II), the band has remained a constant fixture in town. Now with over 100 performing band members, and hundreds of associate members, the New Holland Band plays regular concerts throughout the year, some to standing-room-only crowds.

I found this museum completely by providence. Shop-

ping for a quilt in Lancaster County one Saturday, I inno-
cently drove east on Route 23. At one red light I saw a blue
sign with a picture of a French horn, the word "museum,"
and an arrow pointing to the right. I had to follow it; what
else could I do? Once again, the small museum was calling
my name.

When I walked up the stairs to the second floor of the
Eastern Lancaster County Community Library, I met Luke
Bowman, museum volunteer and my tour guide. Luke came
to New Holland from the Allentown area in 1959 and taught
elementary school band in the local school district until his
retirement in 1996. Now he spends his time volunteering
with the Band Museum.

This museum—stop me if you've heard this before—was
started out of someone's personal collection. Conductor and
band historian Art Futer collected anything band-related:
instruments, sheet music, records, photographs, posters, and
programs. The New Holland Band Museum originally occu-
pied space in the borough hall, but when that building was
sold, the museum relocated to the library.

Everything "band" you can think of is here. Instruments
from bugles to baritones, saxophones to bass drums, both
antique and modern. I saw a one-key flute circa 1725 and a
key bugle from 1820. It's not well known that Pennsylvania
has had a number of instrument manufacturers, too. The
Nuss slide trombone on display was made in Harrisburg and
the Keefer B-flat cornet in Williamsport.

Part of the museum consists of photographs of former
New Holland Band members. Over the years, members
have gone on to bigger and better things, to the Sousa Band

or the U.S. Marine Band. In fact, Luke told me proudly, the chief librarian for the U.S. Marine Band, Michael Ressler, came from New Holland and is a veteran of the band.

While the New Holland community band thrives today, the museum holds reminders of things past. Imagine a night parade without streetlights—torches that were used to illuminate the parade route for the marchers hang on the museum walls. I looked at some handwritten band music from the late 1800s and wondered how the performers could read it. A snare drum head autographed by such notables as Paul Whiteman, Ruby Keeler, and Al Jolson hangs on the wall, as does a drum head used in President John F. Kennedy's funeral procession.

Do many people know that composer and conductor John Philip Sousa, without whom the Fourth of July would not be the same, died in the Abraham Lincoln Hotel in nearby Reading on March 5, 1932? Sousa was scheduled

The New Holland Band Museum

Eastern Lancaster County Library Building
New Holland, PA 17557
(717) 354-5280
www.newhollandband.org

HOURS:
Tuesday and Thursday 2 P.M.–8 P.M., Saturday 10 A.M.–4 P.M.

DIRECTIONS:
From Route 23, turn south on Kinzer Avenue. Turn left on East Jackson Street (right after the railroad tracks). Turn right on Park Avenue. The library/museum is on the left.

to conduct a concert the next day. The baton he last used in rehearsal was retrieved and is now on display in the museum.

I saw many familiar town names on my tour: Ringgold Band from Reading; Allentown Band, "finest in the state," according to Luke; the Red Hill Band, near Perkiomen; Wyomissing Band; the Spring Garden Band, from York. The Winona Band from Shillington is now gone, as is Reg Kehoe and His All-Girl Marimba Band. I'm really sorry I missed that last one.

When I started writing this book, I heard there was a Streitwieser Foundation Trumpet Museum in Pottstown. It advertised "more than 700 trumpets, tubas, trombones and other brass instruments, spanning 3,000 years." When it came time for me to tour it, though, that museum was gone without a trace. Luke Bowman solved the mystery of its disappearance for me. He said that the museum owner/collector had moved—lock, stock, and trombone—back to his native Switzerland.

The Streitwieser departure makes the New Holland Band Museum a little more precious. The only other instrument display I found in the state was at the Moravian Archives Museum in Lititz, but they don't have the other items like sheet music, posters, and drum heads. If you are at all interested in music, the New Holland Band Museum is a great destination.

Toy Robot Museum

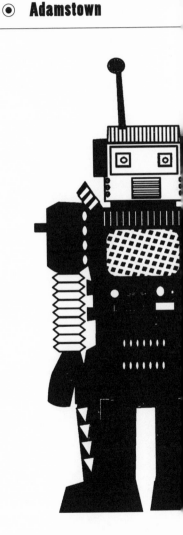

The story of why a small museum exists can be as interesting as the collection itself. The Toy Robot Museum certainly sounds like a fun place—and it is—but the inspiration for it came from a real-life situation.

Joe Knedlhans was a New York City policeman, part of the NYPD's hazardous duty force. For their safety, officers relied on Remotec, a $95,000 robot. Equipped with taser, shotgun, video camera, and microphone, Remotec was sent into hostile situations instead of or before human police officers. In honor of Joe's "partner," his wife, Margo, began giving Joe robots as gifts—and the collection was born. When Joe retired from the force, he and Margo moved to Adamstown, a place they had seen while antiquing over the years, and opened the Toy Robot Museum.

One Saturday afternoon, my friend Joyce and I walked through the "quaint European village" known as Stoudtburg, next to the Black Angus Antique Mall in Adamstown. It seemed an unlikely place for any kind of futuristic-minded robot museum. Small signs guided us past many identical, vacant buildings and we wondered where we were headed.

But a cheerful red robot standing outside the museum let us know we had arrived.

Tours through the museum are self-guided, but Joe was more than happy to spend time talking to us about his collection. The first thing to catch my eye was the Rock 'Em, Sock 'Em Robots. Joe has four of them, with one prominently placed within reach. The sign on it invites visitors "Play with me!" Oh, if only we'd had more time! I never had one of those toys as a child—after all, I was a *girl*—but the kid across the street did and I got to go a round or two with him occasionally.

If those little plastic popping heads weren't enough of a memory jolt, Joe showed us the little audioplayers that were attached to some display cases. He pressed one button and I heard, "He knocked my block off!" The Rock 'Em, Sock 'Em Robot TV commercial—I know it so well.

Other friendly faces greeted us as we walked from case to case. I always had a weak spot for the Lost in Space robot (he really did carry the show) and there he was, in a number of sizes. The motion-activated version even says, "Danger, Danger, Will Robinson!" I wasn't aware that he got work after *Lost in Space*, but the museum has a card ad for Altoids mints with his likeness. Curious.

Robots—where would science fiction movies be without them? The museum has a model of Maria, the first female robot, from the silent movie *Metropolis* (1927). Robby the Robot appeared in *Forbidden Planet* (1956) and later had a few guest spots on *Lost in Space*. He's there. The *Star Wars* collection (1978–) contains probably the most famous present-day robots; I was amused to see a C3Po head wearing an

Deep in the Lower Susquehanna Valley

R2D2 mask. It would never be the other way around.

Some of the toy robots broke new technological ground. Robert the Robot, made in 1954, was the first American-made talking toy. The educational My Friend Talking Toby uses cards with bar codes to operate; the 2XL has an eight-track tape deck. A far cry from today's Furby and microchips.

The walls of the museum are lined with lit cases, just crammed full of robots. Don't look for astronauts; Joe made

it clear he doesn't collect them. But you will find dogs, birds, chickens, dinosaurs, all in robot form. He told us we were only seeing half of the entire collection of 3,500 pieces. Hard as it is to imagine, he says he has "as much packed away as is here." Some of his robots are going to be loaned to a museum in New York, but there are plenty more to fill in.

This is totally a kid-friendly place. While I was there, some parents came in with a seven-year-old and unleashed him in the museum. Joe took it in stride, pausing to answer any of the boy's unending questions with patience and good humor. Even "What is your most expensivest thing?" didn't phase him. The answer to that question, by the way, is Topo, the Androbot (android robot). Created by Atari founder Nolan Bushnell, Topo was the first house robot and has the unfortunate fate of requiring an Apple computer to operate.

The Toy Robot Museum is a great way to spend an afternoon, wandering back through your memory or forward in your imagination. Play pinball, play with the Rock 'Em, Sock 'Em, test Joe's knowledge on his collection. This one is just plain fun.

Toy Robot Museum

9 Market Plaza
Adamstown, PA 19501
(717) 484-0809
www.thetoyrobotmuseum.com

HOURS:
Friday–Sunday 10 a.m.–5 p.m.

DIRECTIONS:
From the Lancaster/Reading exit of the Pennsylvania Turnpike, go straight. Turn right on Route 272 North. Turn left just before Black Angus Antique Mall. The museum is in the village on the left.

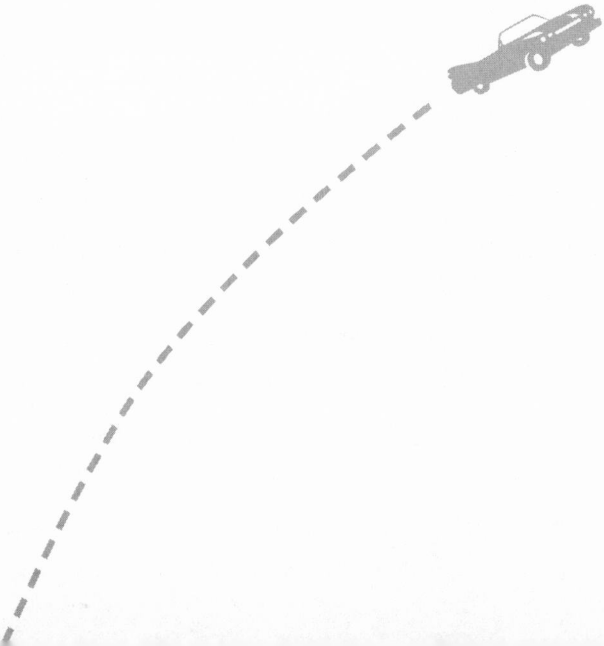

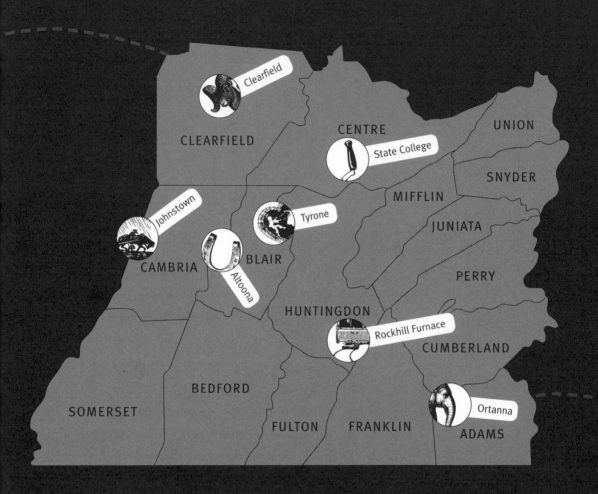

CLEARFIELD

Clearfield

CENTRE

State College

UNION

SNYDER

MIFFLIN

JUNIATA

Johnstown

Tyrone

CAMBRIA

BLAIR

Altoona

PERRY

HUNTINGDON

Rockhill Furnace

CUMBERLAND

BEDFORD

Ortanna

SOMERSET

FULTON

FRANKLIN

ADAMS

HEART OF THE ALLEGHENIES

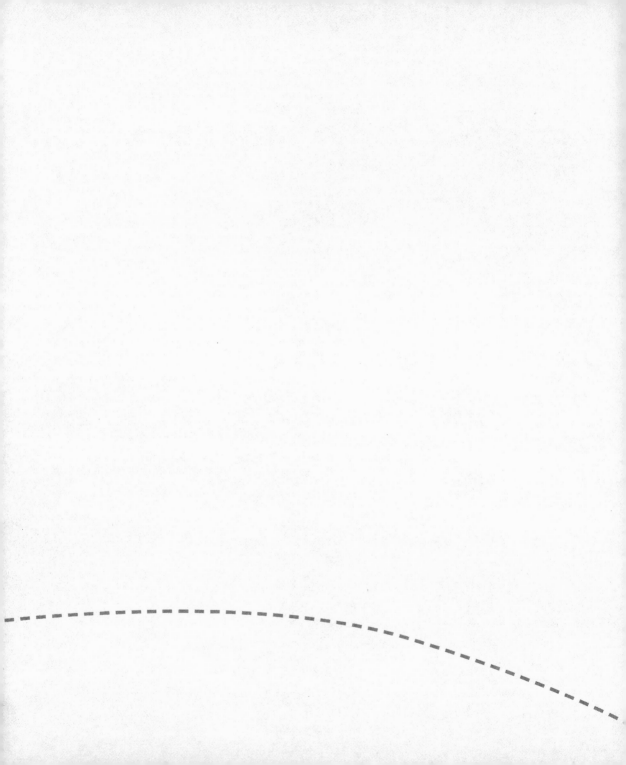

Gardners Candies

What is it about chocolate? The flavor? The fragrance? The little rush you get from indulging? It's hard to imagine that chocolate as we know it hasn't been around all that long, that people survived without this sweet creamy luxury for thousands of years. But we're making up for it now. Did you ever think you'd live to see the day when chocolate would be called good for us? That day has finally come.

Pennsylvania is fortunate to be rich with chocolate makers. Of course, the name Milton Hershey needs no elaboration. But other, smaller, candymakers all across the state have their own loyal followers. People literally line up in Lititz for the little bites of bliss that are Wilbur Buds. A quick search of the Internet brings up chocolate candymakers in Trumbauersville, Mountainhome, and York. And if it wasn't for James Gardner, the world would never have known the Meltaway, a chocolate-enrobed peanut-butter candy bar that truly melts in your mouth.

James "Pike" Gardner started his candy business in 1897 at the age of sixteen. A true entrepreneur looking for ways to increase sales, Gardner bought a wagon so that he could sell candy, popcorn, and peanuts at local fairs and carnivals (sort of a nineteenth-century Mr. Ed—see Mr. Ed's Elephant Museum). From those beginnings, Gardners Candies stores spread all over Pennsylvania like a milk chocolate bar on a warm summer's day.

For all his hard work, Gardner ought to be more famous than he is. After all, he gave Valentine's Day a boost matched only by Hallmark and FTD. Gardner is credited with creating the heart-shaped candy box. Roses are nice, but what would February 14 be without that bright-red heart full of chocolate? Just another cold winter day.

Although there are many Gardners Candies' stores through the region, the Gardners museum can only be found in one place: Tyrone. Its quaint downtown was lively the morning we visited, with many shoppers on the street. My traveling companion was my friend Patty. For once I didn't need to explain the reason for my destination. I would have had no problem getting friends or relatives—or strangers, for that matter—to volunteer for this trip.

We parked on the street and were easily lured inside by the distinctive aroma that pervades and surrounds all Gardners stores—I don't know what it is, sort of sweet, sort of warm and comforting, definitely good. The museum room divides the candy section of the store from the ice-cream parlor. Temptation everywhere you turn.

Our tour started with a short video on the candy-making process at the Gardners Candies factory, which is located in another part of Tyrone. I miss the old days of live factory tours, like the chocolate-making plant at Hershey, but to the best of my knowledge there are no chocolate factories that let you in anymore. Some say it's for safety reasons, others say it's the need to protect company secrets. Sitting on a homey wooden bench at Gardners, we had the next best thing: in the video we saw how Gardners' vanilla creams are carefully made. And while the ever-mysterious Meltaways were mentioned, no classified information was divulged. Guess we won't be making them at home.

The rest of the museum consists of items relating to the company's history and the making of candy. James Gardner's original sales wagon is preserved, as is one of the store's first cash registers. An early 1900s ice cream freezer, a dipping table, and huge copper kettles give an idea of the size of equipment needed to make these wonderful treats. Gardners also has candy molds and antique tin boxes, and plenty of candy advertising items.

My favorite case, of course, holds the large display of heart-shaped candy boxes. Romance just exudes from these boxes, in a rainbow of colors, some plain, some decorated with ribbons, bows, and flowers. Made my heart beat faster

Gardners Candies

30 West 10th Street
Tyrone, PA 16686
(814) 684-0857
www. gardnerscandies.com

HOURS:

Monday–Saturday 9:30 A.M.–
9 P.M., Sunday 1 P.M.–9 P.M.

DIRECTIONS:

Take Route 322 to the Tyrone exit.
Turn left on Pennsylvania Avenue
and right on Tenth Street. Gardners is on the right near the end
of the block.

THE BEST PLACES YOU'VE NEVER SEEN

Heart of the Alleghenies

(or was it the smell of chocolate wafting from the next room?).

The museum also covers some of the history of Tyrone, with milk bottles from local dairies and a cigar box from a Tyrone cigar manufacturer. Copies of 1785 Tyrone land grants are on display. You may not be aware that on May 30, 1893, the Walter L. Mains Circus Train derailed in nearby Bald Eagle. Photographs on the museum walls document the event, which if Fox News had been around then would have been called "the wreck of the century."

Gardners isn't the only chocolate museum in the state. Hershey has a museum with a section dedicated to chocolate making. Wilbur's in Lititz has an impressive chocolate pot display. I chose Gardners, though, because tucked into the mountains as it is, it might be overlooked in any chocolate tour of Pennsylvania.

In case you're thinking of avoiding this place because it may not fit into your diet, remember that chocolate is now considered good for you. It wasn't that long ago that it was believed to cause acne. Now the word used is "antioxidant," as in cancer-fighter. For a full account of chocolate's good side, visit the Chocolate Manufacturers Association's website at www.candyusa.org.

I have no doubt that museum visitors will be tempted to indulge after their tour, so drive carefully when you leave. While as of this writing the Pennsylvania State Police have not yet developed the chocolate breathalyzer, you never know. When we were pulled over for speeding on a back road to State College, I thought I might have to use the "chocolate-covered Oreo defense," but we were sent on our way with just a warning. Thank you, Trooper Inlow!

Grice's Clearfield Community Museum

As is true for a large part of Pennsylvania, in Clearfield County the Monday after Thanksgiving is sacred. It's the first day of buck season. Adults take off work and schools close. Boys (and even some girls) learn how to hunt and trap, skin, and prepare game. Taxidermy is considered an art form. And here, in Clearfield, is a museum dedicated to that "art."

Grice's Clearfield Community Museum is—I have to say it—a *man's* museum: wall-to-wall cars and game, game and cars. The museum is stuffed with game mounts—nearly 400, both "full" (the whole animal) and "shoulder" (wall hangings)—as well as close to seventy antique cars.

Why would someone combine cars and game in one museum? Simply because they both interest local entrepreneur and Clearfield County native Lynn "Scoot" Grice, the museum's founder. In 1955, just back from serving in the Army, Scoot opened a Sinclair gas station in Clearfield. In 1962 he started Grice Gun Shop, well known among hunters and still in business today.

In the early 1990s, Scoot, by then a local success story, was looking for a way "to give back to the community." Through

his gun shop he knew many, many hunters with prizes and nowhere to display them ("You're not hanging that in here, honey!"). Because he collected automobiles, Scoot knew other car enthusiasts ("... and get that thing out of the driveway, too!"). The idea for the museum was born. But I shouldn't give away the whole tale. You can read Scoot's autobiography for yourself—it's on sale in the museum gift shop.

In his museum, Scoot makes sure to honor his humble beginnings. To reach the display area Patty and I had to pass through an exact replica of the Sinclair station that started it all, complete with gas pumps. Any kid who thinks all gas stations also sell lottery tickets, toilet paper, and cigarettes is going to be amazed. This tiny building wouldn't hold the bottled water display now in your local minimarket.

Once we stepped through the Sinclair station, we were nearly in "the wide open spaces." Before us lay a gigantic warehouse—25,000 square feet—of virtually nothing but taxidermized animals and antique cars. We headed down the carpeted path, past Cadillacs and Chevys, armadillos and brown bears, Cougars and cougars. Even a cardboard stand-up of Marilyn Monroe. Since the tour is self-guided, we had plenty of time to look at everything carefully. Every turn brought something new—around one corner I found myself eyeball to eyeball with a kangaroo. (He looked as surprised as I was.) I won't describe the "hootenanny mount"; you'll have to see that for yourself.

It's a good thing the animals are labeled because they are not always easy to identify. This is not just a bunch of white-tail deer mounts from someone's rec room. Fish, fowl, bears of all types—brown, black, grizzly, and polar. Rhino, caribou, bison, blue wildebeest, Iranian sheep, dik diks, and Southern Great Kudu—animals most people in this state have never seen alive.

All the game mounts are donated ("Yes, dear, the museum would be a wonderful place for it"). Some displays are accompanied by brief histories of the owners. A tribute to local resident Bill Evans, who took five hunting trips to Africa, as well as to Alaska and British Columbia, dominates one corner of the museum. Before his death from cancer in

"I've been here FIFTY SOME YEARS AND THIS TOWN'S BEEN good to me."

—Lynn "Scoot" Grice

1993, Evans presented his entire collection, including a full-size African lion, to Grice, saying he wanted a "good home" for his collection.

Each car has an identification label, but car lovers will recognize most of them anyway. Showpieces include a '94 Dodge Viper and a '32 Rockne Six. Boomer motorheads will appreciate the '68 Camaro, the '57 T-Bird, and the '70 Super Bee. While a number of the cars are Scoot's, others are on loan from local car collectors. I was amused to see the

Burma-Shave signs, but children may need to have them explained.

It hasn't always been smooth sailing for Grice's. Tragedy struck in March 1994 when the building collapsed from the weight of snow and ice on the roof. Many cars were damaged, but only three were too far gone to be restored. The museum was closed for a full year while repairs were made. One car owner now keeps his smashed vehicle on display as a monument to the event.

While there are other car museums in the state (such as Jerry's Classic Cars in Pottsville and the Antique Automobile Club of America in Hershey), this is the only one where you can get your fill of game as well. (And, of course, vice-versa.) There is a Wildlife and Whitetail Museum at the Double Diamond Deer Ranch on Route 36 in Cook Forest, but that's a little farther off the beaten path.

Maybe I should have brought someone who hunts or likes cars (Patty has eaten venison and she can pump her own gas, but that's about it). Despite the fact that we were strangers to this culture, we had a good time wandering through the museum, occasionally gasping or giggling as we went. Boring it is not.

The word *museum* conjures up thoughts of "works of art" or "historical artifacts," not a 1968 VW with a Rolls Royce front or a blond caribou. So maybe someone might want to call this a "dead wild animal park" or "auto show." Don't let the "museum" label turn you off. Anyone interested in hunting, wildlife, or cars would thoroughly enjoy Grice's. But it is definitely not the place to take your friends in PETA.

Grice's Clearfield Community Museum

119 N. Fourth Street
Clearfield, PA 16830
(814) 768-7332

HOURS:
Summer only. Monday–Thursday, Saturday 10 A.M.–4 P.M., Friday 10 A.M.–8 P.M., and Sunday 1 P.M.–4 A.M.

RESTRICTIONS:
No one under 16 is admitted without an adult.

DIRECTIONS:
From Interstate 80, take Exit 18 or 19 to Clearfield (Exit 18, Route 153, has some great views of the mountains). From either exit you will find yourself on Route 322, which leads to Third Street. Take Third Street to Pine and make a left. Make another left on Fourth Street. The museum is on the right.

Horseshoe Curve

To some people, vacation means lying on a beach for a week; for others, camping in the mountains. But for a select group nothing could be better than spending a vacation sitting on a park bench waiting for a train.

Of course, that's if the bench is at Horseshoe Curve. Any time of day, any time of year, you'll find these "trainiacs," cameras on their laps, sitting and chatting among themselves while watching the empty train tracks curved tight against the mountain.

Horseshoe Curve—known as the "Amphitheater of the Alleghenies"—has been one of my favorite "small" destinations since I was a child. It's fancier now than it ever has been in its history, though still "small." It's also a National Historic Landmark.

To get to the Curve, my niece Annie and I drove through an Altoona neighborhood known to locals as Eldorado (pronounce that "el-dor-AY-do"), just outside the city limits, and headed up the narrow Kittaning Point Road. Houses that dotted the roadside soon disappeared and our scenery became reservoirs to the left and tree-covered mountain to the right. After one final tight bend in the road, we arrived in the parking lot tucked into the base of the mountain, just below the Curve.

As we got out of the car, I told Annie to look up behind the visitors' center. When the trees lining the railroad tracks are trimmed, you can see any trains wrapped around the mountainside, chugging away on the horseshoe-shaped Curve. The longer the train, the more impressive the sight. I have always liked being able to see the engine and the caboose of a long train at the same time. The tracks were empty when we got there but I knew it wouldn't be long.

Two buildings sit below the Curve, the gift shop and a small museum known as the Visitors' Center, devoted to the building of this "engineering marvel." A package deal for admission that includes the Railroaders Memorial Museum in downtown Altoona is available, but we opted for only the Curve. If you have more time, go ahead—take the package.

So what's the big deal about Horseshoe Curve? Trains have always been able to carry heavy loads. But because they run smooth steel wheels on smooth steel rails, trains lose traction on too steep a grade. In the mid-1800s, when the Pennsylvania Railroad was faced with the problem of how to cross the Allegheny Mountains at a place level enough to operate a train safely, the idea of Horseshoe Curve was born. With only men and hand tools (we're talking picks and shovels here), a link was built between two mountains and across two gorges. Construction of one track was completed on February 15, 1854. Eventually three other tracks were added.

Displays inside the one-room museum include "Building the Curve" and "The Men Who Built the Curve." Many photographs and drawings illustrate how the Curve was designed and built. A large topographical map shows the Curve in relation to the landscape. Since we had just visited the Johnstown Flood Museum, we located that on the map as well. In an adjoining room, a videotape on the building of the Curve runs continuously.

News clippings on display remind visitors of a time when Horseshoe Curve was big news. It was seen as such a threat to the Nazi war effort that Adolf Hitler sent agents here to bomb it; they were captured before they could carry out their plan. Over the years, many prominent individuals, including Thomas Edison, Henry Ford, and numerous presidents, have ridden the train around the Curve.

Although it's not as good as being there, you can find a lot of material about the Horseshoe Curve on the Internet. Trainiacs have many websites, with some devoted solely to photographs of the Curve. The best I found for both history and photographs is the National Railway Historical Society site,

Horseshoe Curve chapter, at http://www.trainweb.org/horse-shoecurve-nrhs/Altoona_area.htm.

The museum's detailed history of the Curve is interesting for adults, but it won't hold most children's attention for very long. Eleven-year-old Annie's favorite part was pushing buttons on the wall to hear the sounds of different steam engines. And so we moved on.

Our next stop was up, up to the tracks of the Curve. When I was a child, the only option was walking up the long set of stone steps, and I couldn't understand why my grandfather stayed at the bottom as we ran up to see the trains. You can still walk the 194 steps, but you can also take the funicular, which is like an inclined plane.

Never one to miss a modern convenience, Annie chose the funicular. With one push of a button we were on our way to the top of the Curve to join the trainiacs. At its peak, the Curve saw 168 trains each day, but now that number is down to sixty or seventy. Still, chances were good we would see one.

While we waited (maybe five minutes), Annie ran along the iron fence separating us from the tracks and looked at the Pennsylvania Railroad GP9 engine on display. She didn't believe me when I told her that her uncle Jack and I had played on those very railroad tracks as youngsters (no fence in the 1960s!).

Trainiacs will tell you anything you want to know about the trains. I spoke to a man from the Philadelphia area, who told me that that the GP9 is still running in Philly. He also told me about other railroads, like the Reading (did you think that was just a Monopoly space?), which has its own

Heart of the Alleghenies

museum in Leesport. Pennsylvania has many other small railroad museums worth visiting.

Our conversation was broken up by the crackling of train radio transmissions, which are broadcast so that spectators can listen to the engineers communicate with each other. We heard enough to know the train was coming up from the south. Tension mounted as we all kept our eyes to the right, waiting and waiting. Then it happened—the first sign of a yellow and black Norfolk Southern freight train, chugging its way up the hill.

The trainiacs pulled up their cameras and started filming. Children ran up and down the sidewalk, waving at the engineers and workmen. Best of all, all the train men waved back. For a little while it was like a parade.

We lost sight of the train, and everyone calmed down, a little deflated. But we had only just settled back into our seats when we heard a new voice over the radio. We knew a train would soon be coming from the other direction. Annie and I began to leave after that train came through, but we had only gotten to the bottom of the hill when we heard yet another coming. She was ready to run up the steps to see it pass but instead we waited in the parking lot so we could watch it from below and see both the engine and the caboose at the same time. That made the trip complete.

This is a wonderful piece of Pennsylvania history, one fading all too fast. Don't miss your chance to go wave to the engineer.

Horseshoe Curve

Visitors' Center
Kittaning Point Road
Altoona, PA 16603
www.railroadcity.com

HOURS:

April–October 9:30 A.M.–7:00 P.M. daily; November–March 10:00 A.M–4:30 P.M. Tuesday through Sunday

DIRECTIONS:

From I-99, take the Duncansville Exit for Route 764 and head toward Altoona. Inside the city limits, turn left onto 58th Street. When the road ends, make a left onto Kittaning Point Road, which will lead you right to Horseshoe Curve.

⊙ **Johnstown**

The Johnstown Flood Museum

Johnstown sits in a valley, surrounded by mountains on all sides. The first time I drove through it I said out loud, "No wonder it flooded three times." Twice in the twentieth century heavy rains caused floods in Johnstown. But when people talk about the "Great Johnstown Flood," they mean only one: May 31, 1889, when the dam on man-made Lake Conemaugh broke and flooded fourteen miles of Cambria County, leaving nothing but death and destruction in its path.

The Flood of 1889 is an incredible story, made all the more unbelievable when you know the details. A tragic disaster may not seem like proper museum material, but the Johnstown Flood Museum is about the people of the area, the times in which they lived, and the changes to their lives that came about as a result of the great flood. The museum is located, appropriately, in a building built in 1891, two years after the flood, with money from Pittsburgh millionaire and South Fork Fishing and Hunting Club member Andrew Carnegie.

The story of the Conemaugh dam is tied to the development of the railroad. In short, once the railroad came through and the Horseshoe Curve was complete, the state didn't need its high-mountain water source for the Pennsylvania Canal and the dam was abandoned in the mid-1800s. For a complete historical overview of the importance of the railroad, start with the Allegheny Portage Railroad Museum on Route 22, follow that with a stop at Horseshoe Curve, and then come over to Johnstown for the flood museum.

In 1879 the South Fork Fishing and Hunting Club purchased the Conemaugh reservoir and turned it into "Lake Conemaugh." Pittsburgh's most affluent citizens, such as Henry Clay Frick and Andrew Carnegie, would leave the heat of the city for a summer at the lake. Despite the wealth of club members, maintenance at the club was substandard. Breaks in the dam were haphazardly repaired with logs, mud, brush, tree stumps, and horse manure. It's amazing that the dam lasted as long as it did.

And then it rained for two solid weeks. Johnstown was doomed when the dam finally gave way on May 31. In all, 2,209 people died; 99 entire families were wiped out and four square miles of woods, towns, and homes were destroyed.

At the center of the museum is a large diorama showing the entire valley. A time line along the side lights up at each stage. I watched it cycle through three times—and this wasn't my first visit. I suspect I'm not the only one who stands there staring at the lights, listening to the sounds, trying to imagine what it must have been like. At 3:10 p.m. on May 31 the dam broke. At 4:07 p.m. the wall of water hit Johnstown, home to 30,000 people.

Every story has its heroes. Many people were saved from the flood because a train engineer coming down the valley heard it coming behind him. He blew his whistle in warning

"HANDS OF THE DEAD STUCK OUT from the ruins."

—Quote from a witness

until the water caught up to the train and swept it away. The diorama lights up the train's path as a train whistle blows.

People haven't changed all that much in 100 years, for either good or bad. The day after the flood tourists came in from Altoona to see the damage, a full day before relief supplies arrived from Pittsburgh. The tourists collected souvenirs, including a bottle of flood water that now on display in the museum. (Who knows what would have turned up if eBay had existed back then?) But once the rescue effort began, people from all over the world pitched in, sending money and goods. Clara Barton and the Red Cross came on June 5 and stayed for five months.

The museum tells the entire story of the flood, from the importance of the railroad to the rebuilding of the community. Chilling photographs show the shock on flood victims' faces, the destruction to what had been Johnstown. Articles of clothing, a pitcher, a kitchen chair—all these things survived the flood and are on display. Another, more enduring monument to both the flood and the people can be found in town. Johnstown's Conemaugh Valley Memorial Hospital was the city's first public hospital, built with the last of the flood relief funds in 1892.

Despite everything that has happened in the world since, the Johnstown Flood remains a significant part of American culture. Even if they don't know the specifics, most people know that it happened. I watched a video of a silent movie from 1926—with the flood as its theme—alternating with a Mighty Mouse cartoon. Of course, in the movie the hero rescues the maiden, and in the cartoon Mighty Mouse saves all the mice. The flood was even mentioned in an Archie comic from the 1960s.

The dam site is still visible at the Johnstown Flood National Memorial in St. Michael's. This quick trip up Route 219 makes the story complete. The Memorial Visitors' Center has survivors' stories on tape and a thirty-five-minute film on the flood.

My niece Annie took this trip with me. She was clearly disturbed by the theme and spent most of her time in the gift shop. Other children wandering through the displays with their parents seemed to have no trouble, but it's not for everyone. I know I won't forget those faces anytime soon.

The Johnstown Flood Museum

304 Washington Street
Johnstown, PA 15901
(814) 539-1889
www.jaha.org/flood

HOURS:
May 1–October 31: Sunday–Thursday, 10 A.M.–4 P.M.; Friday–Saturday 10 A.M.–7 P.M. November 1–April 30: daily, 10 A.M.–5 P.M.

DIRECTIONS:
Take Route 56 into Johnstown. Turn right on Walnut Street. At third stoplight, turn right onto Washington Street. The museum is on the right.

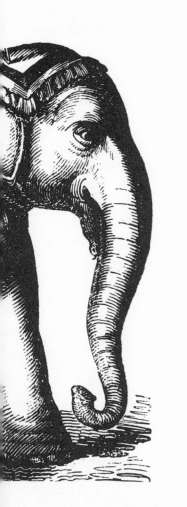

Mr. Ed's Elephant Museum

Mr. Ed's Elephant Museum is one of those places that as a kid you would have begged your parents to take you to on every trip down Route 30. You'd read those brightly colored billboards that beckon—no, nearly command—you to "stop at Mr. Ed's Elephant Museum!" and you'd plead, "Can we?" And when they ignored that request, you'd venture to add, "But it's a *museum*. It's *educational*." Your parents would drive on without a word and you'd be left in the back seat, pining for whatever Mr. Ed's had in store for those lucky kids with more adventurous parents.

Considering those colorful signs, the wooden building known as Mr. Ed's Elephant Museum is surprisingly nondescript, tucked off the side of Route 30 so well that I didn't know where it was until I went looking for it. What did catch my eye, though, was Miss Ellie, a ten-foot-tall plastic elephant who stands out front, beckoning people to Mr. Ed's. She'll speak if she knows you're there (and if they have her switch turned on inside, of course).

Just another tourist trap? Not nearly. Mr. Ed's is a snack and souvenir shop, it's true, but one room is devoted entirely to elephantania (elephernalia? elephantasia?). Visitors are welcome to wander through the museum for as long as they care to at no charge. Over 6,000 elephants of all sorts reside here, all from Mr. Ed's personal collection.

Yes, there really is a Mr. Ed, and he is not the least bit horse-like. A native of York, Pa., Ed Gotwalt started Mr. Ed's in 1975 and moved to his present location in 1983. This cheerful man credits his success merely to "serendipity and fate." Those words pretty much sum up Mr. Ed's entire career. His elephant collection was started for him when his new sister-in-law gave him two elephants as a wedding present in 1967. Mr. Ed and his wife picked up two more on the honeymoon and now, he admits with a straight face, he has "tons of them."

His peanut-selling business also started by chance, when a man drove up to Mr. Ed's with a peanut roaster on the back of his truck. Without much of a sales pitch, Mr. Ed bought the peanut roaster and now sells 15 to 20 tons of peanuts a year.

This elephantine infatuation keeps Mr. Ed very busy. He takes time to speak at local schools and public events so that people can learn about these special animals. The museum ceiling is covered with children's letters thanking him for visiting their schools. My favorite says, "I like you comeing. Elephant ways 3,000 pounds." So ha! to parents everywhere. It *is* educational! Just not for learning spelling.

When Mr. Ed is not selling snacks or speaking in classrooms, he performs in local little theater. While you might

"SHOPLIFTERS WILL BE trampled"

—Sign at Mr. Ed's

Miss Ellie and Mr. Ed.

think that elephants are his first love, "Broadway is my passion," he says with a smile, pointing to a wall of his museum covered with actors' eight-by-tens. He told me about meeting Mandy Patinkin at the railroaders' show in York a few years ago.

With a nod to an elephant celebrity of sorts, Mr. Ed's displays newspaper clippings highlighting the story of Lucy the Elephant. Sixty-five feet high and over 90 tons, Lucy was built in 1881 as an attraction for a real estate developer in what is now Margate, N.J. She's had an uneasy history but now belongs to the city of Margate, which is working to preserve Lucy in the grandeur she was intended for (see www.lucytheelephant.org for her complete history).

Keep in mind that this is a personal collection, almost all elephants given as gifts to Mr. Ed. Visitors can't expect to learn the difference between Asian and African elephants (parents, forget I said that). Those on display have no labels giving origin or date or anything else about them. Mr. Ed says he started to label them, but the chore brought him so many sweet memories he had to stop.

Fortunately, most of the pieces are self-explanatory. Of course there is a full case devoted to the Grand Old Party's contribution to elephant-mania. But during my visit I also saw cookie jars, stacked elephants, baby elephants, cups, snow globes, glass, ceramic, plaster, and metal elephants, mobiles, cookie cutters, boxes, banks, incense holders, a fake elephant nose, salt and pepper shakers, ads for everything from scanners to biscuits, games, records, hot pads, planters, slippers, pins, necklaces, earrings, belts, a lamp, post-it notes, a snack server, books, and lots more. If you can name it, and it ever had an elephant on it, Mr. Ed probably has it.

The only real elephant parts are tusks from an elephant who had died a natural death and some pieces of 100-year-old ivory. Mr. Ed refuses to add any more since he strongly believes that "only elephants should wear ivory."

Educational or not, this is a fun place to stop. Even non-elephant collectors can find something interesting to see, and the peanuts are great.

Mr. Ed's Elephant Museum

6019 Chambersburg Road
Orrtanna, PA 17353
(717) 352-3792
www.mistereds.com

HOURS:
Daily 10 A.M.–5 P.M.

DIRECTIONS:
Mr. Ed's is on Route 30 between Gettysburg and Chambersburg, just west of the intersection of Routes 234 and 30.

Pasto Agricultural Museum

B.C. does not always mean what you think. At the Pasto Agricultural Museum, "B.C." means "before computers." Shuddering yet? How about "B.E."—before electricity or engines? It's so easy to forget (at least until the power goes out) that there were ever days before what we know as "modern conveniences." That's why places like the Pasto exist—to remind us of how far we've come.

I drove out Route 45 one hot summer day past acres of cornfields, trying to locate the museum. I've always known that these were Penn State cornfields but I didn't realize there were also buildings and research facilities out there behind the corn. Once I found the museum, I also found curator and Penn State professor Dr. Darwin Braund.

Dr. Braund is happy to provide a very good idea of what life was like for our near-ancestors, those who lived before 1940. The museum collection covers many parts of daily life both on the farm and in the home. If you think getting a less-than-fresh cup of coffee at the minimart can ruin your whole day, come to the Pasto and see how good you've got it.

The tour starts with the farm life, preparing the land,

planting, and harvesting. Dr. Braund said, "For centuries, the most important event on earth was the harvest." He's right, of course—a good harvest meant life, a bad one starvation and possibly death.

Keeping that in mind, I looked at the hand tools used for farming. I saw seeders and sickles, scythes and rakes. I also saw many pieces of large machinery, the kind that would be pulled by livestock. One thing I loved about this museum was that Dr. Braund could start up the equipment. I didn't have to try to imagine how something worked, I saw it in operation, like the self-raking reaper from 1904.

Until the thresher came into existence, grain was gathered by beating the stalks with a flail until the grain came off. Once the thresher was developed, the same result could be achieved more easily. With the addition of a fanning mill, the straw and chaff were separated from the grain at the same

Pasto Agricultural Museum

Russell E. Larson Ag
Research Center
State College, PA 16801
(814) 863-1383
pasto.cas.psu.edu

HOURS:

Tours by appointment, or daily
during Ag Progress Days in
August.

DIRECTIONS:

From State College, take Route 45
west to Entrance K. Turn left,
drive up driveway, and the museum is on the left.

time. Dr. Braund put it in modern terms: "This idea of multi-tasking is not new."

The grain binder (this one circa 1939) had been pulled by two or three horses. It not only gathered the grain but the knotter tied it with twine. A week later, I was very pleased when I recognized a grain binder being used on an Amish farm.

Animals did a lot more than just pull wagons. They were often used to run equipment. The King Thresher, a combination thresher and fanning mill, was horse-powered. Dr. Braund told me about a school group that came through recently and the little girl whose favorite part was "the Nordic track for horses." A smaller treadmill, used to churn butter, could be run by a goat or dog.

From farm equipment we moved into the household section. The early vacuum cleaner with a hand pump didn't look like it would pick up much—no "cyclonic action" here. The gasoline-powered iron just plain scared me. I recognized the oak-roller clothes washer, but I'll stick to my Maytag.

Dr. Braund brought me into the twenty-first century again when he said, "Recycling is not a new concept." He showed me some poultry feed bags that had been made into clothing and told me that these days people collect feedsacks. I have not yet seen the feedsack clothing museum, though, so they must be keeping their collections under control.

Without a doubt, this is a great place for kids to learn what life was like on the farm not all that long ago. Many adults will probably learn a lot as well. If you schedule your visit during Ag Progress Days in August, you'll be able to spend the day and see a whole lot more than the museum.

Rockhill Trolley Museum

Nothing can match the experience of riding a trolley car. While trolleys used to be the urban transportation of choice for much of the twentieth century, these days it's almost impossible to find a real one to ride. It's all buses and light rail now—no clicking, no shifting side to side as the trolley bounces on the tracks, and no sliding across the seat as it rounds a curved track—it's just not the same. Fortunately, Pennsylvania has three trolley museums spread across the state. In far west Washington, Pa., northeast in Scranton, and nearly the center of the state in little Rockhill you can ride to the zing-zing-zing of your hearts' content.

The Rockhill Trolley Museum appealed to me in part because I once lived on Germantown Avenue in Chestnut Hill, where trolleys ran over the cobblestone street day and night. City girl that I am, I enjoyed the clanging, clicking sounds as the trolley passed my apartment. When visitors came, I often made them ride the trolley—not that we were going anywhere, I just wanted to give them the experience. Sadly, I moved away and eventually so did the trolley.

But now I had the chance to show my niece Annie the

wonders of a trolley ride. In the town of Orbisonia, we found the popular and well-advertised East Broad Top Railroad. Across the street (in Rockhill Furnace) is the Rockhill Trolley Museum. There were long lines for the steam trains but none, it seemed, for the trolleys. I couldn't believe no one wanted this rare experience.

As it turned out, however, people did want to ride the trolley. Trolleys depart from the station every half hour and we had just missed one. So we wandered into the museum /gift shop while we waited. The small museum display focuses on the history of the York and Harrisburg trolley line through photographs and descriptions of what used to be. These days even the tracks are gone from those towns.

Rockhill was started by trolley enthusiasts in 1960 looking to preserve a remnant of the glory days. The first trolley car to be displayed at the museum came from Johnstown and still runs today. Devotees travel from all over to volunteer their weekends at the museum, working to restore trolleys in the barn, overseeing tours, and operating the various trolleys. The man who sold us our tickets was a retired truck driver. He told me how people come from as far as Allentown to volunteer. And they're always looking for more hands; when he saw my interest, he tried to recruit me.

The highlight, of course, was the trolley ride. We boarded the York Railways #163, which used to run on East Market Street in York. After the trolley line ended in 1939, this car was used as a vacation home on the banks of the Susquehanna River. Tropical Storm Agnes came through in 1972 and put an end to that. Eventually, the trolley was rescued and came to Rockhill for its next life.

And a glorious life it now has. It's hard to imagine this gorgeous trolley was ever under mucky flood waters. What a beautiful restoration! The woven seats are smooth and comfortable, the polished wooden ceiling a beauty. Why was I surprised to see no graffiti on the advertisements lining the ceiling? It was obvious this refurbishment was a labor of love.

A little maneuvering and we were off. Unlike all my previous trolley rides on city streets, this one would take us two and a half miles through the country. Before this visit I thought trolleys never left the cities. But they often ran between towns, through countryside, sometimes carrying passengers, sometimes freight. As we rode through the trees, it was easy to imagine having a picnic basket and taking a trolley ride to get out of the city heat for a day.

Our trip took us past the remains of the Rockhill Iron Furnace. All the while, the crew members entertained us with history and technical facts about trolleys. We paused at the end of the line, turned our seats around, and headed back. It was too short a ride. When we came to a stop, the driver let Annie step on the air brakes—a highlight for her.

In all the museum has two dozen trolleys, two car barns, a restoration and maintenance shop, and a museum/gift shop. You never know which trolley you'll be riding because the collection varies. It could be an open-air trolley with benches and no sides, or an aluminum trolley from suburban Philadelphia. But you can be sure you'll be among people who love what they do and are very happy to share it with you.

Rockhill Trolley Museum

Route 994
Rockhill Furnace, PA 17249
(814) 447-9576
www.rockhilltrolley.org

HOURS:

Weekends and holidays from Memorial Day weekend through October, 11 A.M.–4 P.M.

DIRECTIONS:

From the Pennsylvania Turnpike, take the Fort Littleton Exit. Follow Route 522 north 25 minutes to Orbisonia. Turn left at the traffic light. Turn left at the railroad tracks (East Broad Top Railroad is on the right).

LAWRENCE

BUTLER

JEFFERSON

ARMSTRONG

BEAVER

INDIANA

Pittsburgh

Pittsburgh

Indiana

ALLEGHENY

Wilmerding

WESTMORELAND

WASHINGTON

GREEN

Uniontown

FAYETTE

IRON CiTY ENVIRONS

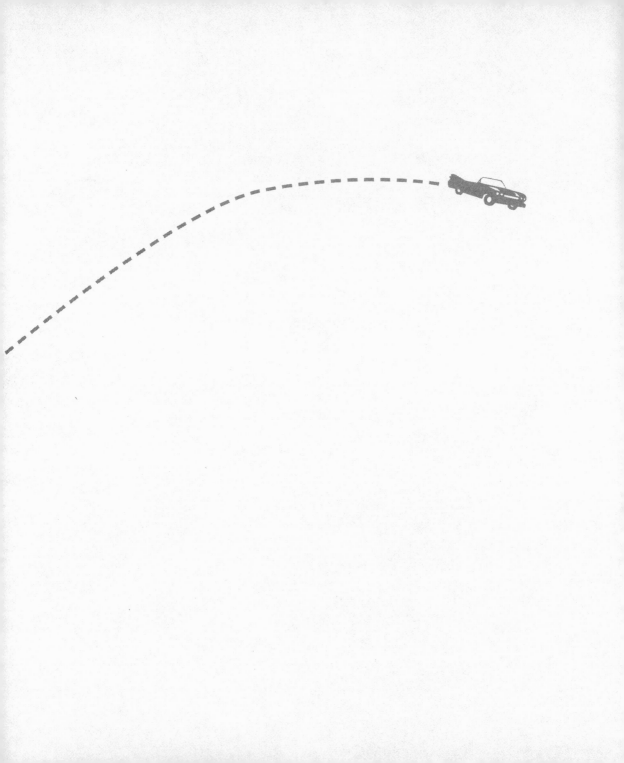

Coal and Coke Heritage Center

You can't drive too far west or north in Pennsylvania without coming across a billboard for a coal-mine tour. The Seldom Seen Mine is in Patton, the Lackawanna in Scranton, the Pioneer Mine in Ashland. Those tours take you deep under the earth to experience a mine first-hand. But—and I'm sure this question is asked often, especially after seventy-seven hours spent watching the Quecreek rescue—what is available for the claustrophobic? Those who dread the thought of being underground, where it's dark and (often) dripping water? Where can they go to learn about coal mining in Pennsylvania without ever entering a confined space?

The Coal and Coke Heritage Center in Uniontown, that's where. On the bottom floor of the library at Penn State University–Fayette sits a bright little museum quietly dedicated to coal mining, especially relating to the McConnellsville Basin and the making of coke. All a visitor has to do to enter the world of mining is walk down a flight of stairs from the first-floor library (or take the elevator).

"Coke?" you say. We're not talking cola here. Or some drug cartel laundering money as a coal-mining operation. In

"WE'RE A MINE OF INFORMATION"

—promotional material for the Coal and Coke Heritage Center

this case, coke is coal that has been baked for three days until almost all the impurities have been removed, making it ideal for the manufacturing of steel. Fayette County in particular was known for its high-quality coking coal. During American steel's heyday, Fayette County benefited greatly from its close proximity to Pittsburgh's steel mills.

Until Quecreek, most likely many people outside Pennsylvania, Kentucky, and West Virginia thought coal mining was a thing of the past. It's true that in the early 1900s nearly 200,000 Pennsylvanians worked in coal mining, and by the end of the century the number was closer to 8,000 workers. But coal mining is still a significant contributor to Pennsylvania's economy. The two most productive coal mines in the world are in Pennsylvania and, according to the Pennsylvania Coal Association, coal is used to produce over half of the electricity generated in Pennsylvania.

While mining has never been known as an easy way to make a living, producing coke was equally difficult. The coal had to be maintained at that 2,200-degree temperature in beehive-shaped ovens for three days. Men who could bake coal into coke were considered to have a special talent. Some could tell exactly how the coal was baking just by sight; any good cook can do the same in a kitchen, but it's not 2,200 degrees for three days! The last of the coke ovens closed in the 1980s but they are still visible in the nearby town of Shoaf.

Project coordinator Pam Seighman was my guide. She explained that the center performs double duty as both a museum and a research center. The research center opened in 1977. As part of its contribution to preserving the coke workers' history, the center published *Patch/Work Voices*, a

book about the workers in the area. During the coke-making years, families lived in what was known as the "Patch," an assortment of neighborhood communities with strong ties to the life of miners and coke workers.

When the center added exhibits in the early 1990s, it became a museum as well. Museum tours are planned

Take Your Daughter to Work Day, 1935. Matthew A. Hunchuck Sr., a driver in the Amend Mine of the Irwin Gas and Coal Company (*left*), and Charles Migyanko Sr. give a ride to Hunchuck's daughter Betty (age 3) and niece Dolores Pansic (5). Mac the pony usually worked in the mine.

according to a group's interests, whether it's schoolchildren learning about mining or a family with a mining background in town for a reunion. It seems the center is not very well known outside southwestern Pennsylvania; I found it only by luck. But it is known internationally by historians and mining operations for its breadth of information.

Much mining equipment is on display. The miner's hat has evolved from a soft cloth one, to a turtle-shell shape, to the present-day hard hat with a fan in the back to keep the miner a little cooler. Other items miners carried and used daily are included: lunch buckets, detonators, dynamite boxes, respirators, and safety lamps. If you've seen the movie *October Sky*, you already know what the brass checks are used for.

I came up with some new vocabulary on this visit. I always wondered about those little buildings with conveyor belts at coal mines. They're called "tipples." These buildings sit over mine shafts. The coal is raised up from the mine through the tipple and down a chute into the ovens to be baked. The museum has a wooden scale model of a tipple, as well as many paintings and drawings. I guess it makes a more attractive picture than a mine shaft.

I was very moved by the personal side of this museum. Touring a coal mine gives you an idea of what it was like to work underground. But what was life like above ground for these miners? How did the families live? A large part of the museum is dedicated to the miners' family life. Clothing and cooking utensils are featured, as are pictures of husbands, wives, and children who lived and breathed mining.

Coal mining is such a deep part of Pennsylvania's heritage that practically everyone knows someone who knows someone who was a miner. Pam said that families often come in, asking about a relative or a particular mine. The museum has no personal records on miners, unless a worker was seriously injured or killed. But they are quite happy to talk in general about what a company was like, or what conditions were like for miners.

There are many worthwhile mining museums in the state, each with its own personality. Understandably, the Quecreek rescue capsule, which will soon be on display at Windber's Coal Heritage Center, will draw a lot of attention. But if you're looking for a complete picture of mining—the people and the work—be sure to stop at the Coal and Coke Heritage Center.

Coal and Coke Heritage Center

Fayette Campus
Penn State University
Route 119
Uniontown, PA 15401
(724) 430-4158
www.coalandcoke.org

HOURS:

Monday–Friday 10 A.M.–3 P.M., and by appointment.

DIRECTIONS:

From the Pennsylvania Turnpike, exit at New Stanton and travel 21 miles south on Route 119 to the Fayette Campus. The Coal and Coke Heritage Center is located on the ground floor of the Fayette Campus Library.

George Westinghouse Museum

The Westinghouse name probably brings to mind washers and dryers, maybe refrigerators. Definitely household appliances. Radio or TV commercials? "Every house needs Westinghouse" or "You can be *sure* if it's Westinghouse." But George Westinghouse did a lot more than make housework a breeze. He also stopped trains and lit up the night.

Inventor and entrepreneur George Westinghouse Jr. (1846–1914) was one of those kids who tinkered with whatever he could put his hands on. By the time he was twenty Westinghouse had a patent for a rotary steam engine. Just a few years later he developed the air brake, which allowed trains to stop without coasting a long distance first, thereby preventing many an accident. His air-brake invention would only be the first of countless achievements for George Westinghouse.

From the Westinghouse Air Brake Company to the Union Switch and Signal Company and the Philadelphia Company (a natural-gas supplier), the Westinghouse empire grew. Westinghouse mastered the use of alternating-current electricity and brought a new kind of power into people's homes.

Bertha Lamme worked for Westinghouse Electric & Manufacturing Company from 1893 to 1905. She was a very talented engineer at a time when women were not hired to work as engineers.

To demonstrate the safety of this new invention, he supplied the lighting for the World's Columbian Exposition in 1893. By the time he died in 1914, George Westinghouse truly was a household name.

The George Westinghouse Museum is housed inside "the Castle," a grand stone edifice that served as the headquarters for the Westinghouse Air Brake Company. There's no confusing the Castle for any other building in Wilmerding; you'll see it rising well above all those little Western Pennsylvanian rowhomes.

The museum was started by Charles Rich (1918–98), a Westinghouse employee and historian who felt the need to recognize the achievements of Westinghouse, both the man and the company. Like a lot of company museums I visited, many items here were donated by former employees, such as the bronzed work shoes of a forty-year Westinghouse worker.

The museum is organized within four rooms, beginning with the Westinghouse family's belongings. Looking around, it's hard to keep the Georges straight. Since George Jr., the inventor, there have been three others: George III, George Thomas, and George IV. Some of their belongings are on display in the Family Room. Beautiful glasses and plates, some Tiffany, show what it was like to be a wealthy family in the Victorian age. I could picture a servant carrying that elaborate silver coffee service into a room to serve guests or Mrs. Westinghouse unpacking her travel trunk just home from the Continent.

The Invention Room contains, of course, George Westinghouse Jr.'s inventions, with full descriptions on printed cards. Most of the details were lost on me; I'm just not mechanically inclined. I noticed two Czech engineering students in the Inventions Room while I was visiting. From the guest book, I could tell that they had been in there for two and a half hours. Obviously, they understood mechanical things better than I do.

In the Room of Achievement my interest picked up. This is the largest and most varied room in the museum. Although I take the radio I listen to every day for granted, it still thrilled me to hear the recording of the first radio broadcast ever, which came from Pittsburgh's KDKA. I can't help but think it must have seemed magical for the first people who heard radio. That room also contains replicas of the 1938 and 1965 time capsules buried at the World's Fair. They're not to be opened until 6939; that I couldn't fathom either.

My favorite was the Appliance Room. My "Little Suzy Homemaker" side came right out when I saw the ironer, which did shirts in a mere six minutes! Can someone explain to me why an early iron was called a "mangle"? Sounds like clothes would come out worse than they went in. The Laundromat was the first automatic washer that didn't have to be bolted to the floor; I guess that's progress. A 1925 electric range, a 1935 refrigerator, and a 1948 crockpot—after looking at them, you can bet I'm grateful for my Cuisinart and microwave.

All the companies created by Westinghouse and his successors are now gone. In 1998 an era ended when the Westinghouse Electric Corporation became the CBS Corporation on the New York Stock Exchange. But the museum is a monument to both what used to be and how we got to where we are today.

George Westinghouse Museum

Castle Main
325 Commerce Street
Wilmerding, PA 15148
(412) 823-0500
www.georgewestinghouse.com/museum.html

HOURS:
Monday–Saturday 10 A.M.–4 P.M.

DIRECTIONS:
Take Exit 6 of the Pennsylvania Turnpike and stay in the left lane for Business Route 22. Turn left onto Route 148 (Mosside Blvd.). At the foot of the hill, cross the bridge, turn right onto Wall Avenue, and go two miles to Wilmerding. Follow Station Street to Herman Aveenue. Turn left on Herman. As you turn left again on Commerce Street, the Castle is in full view. Parking around perimeter of the Castle.

Jimmy Stewart Museum

Snow was falling lightly as I parked my car behind the Indiana Library on an early winter's day. Not like the soapflake snowstorm where George Bailey found Clarence, but then this wasn't Bedford Falls either. It was real snow and I was in Indiana, Pa., headed to the Jimmy Stewart Museum, a place I have passed by many times but never before visited.

Entrance to the museum honoring Indiana's most famous native son is through the side door to the town library (no, "She's just about to close up the library!" did not come to mind) and down a few stairs. In the hallway leading to the elevator for the museum is the "It's a Wonderful Life Gallery," with posters and other memorabilia from the movie. The town's fondness for Jimmy Stewart is indisputable. The walls are covered with murals of Bedford Falls and the Granville House, where George and Mary Bailey lived. The murals were painted by local artist Linda Pepper to commemorate the fiftieth anniversary of the film in 1997.

Before getting on the elevator I paused to read some of the studio memos about *It's a Wonderful Life*. Obviously, the

Home from World War II, Jimmy Stewart sits in his father's hardware store.

censors thought this movie was fraught with questionable behavior and salacious language and they wanted to keep a firm lid on it. How else could you explain: "The word 'jerk' is unacceptable" or "Uncle Billy will take a nip on page 86." I laughed the whole way to the third floor.

The museum is far larger than I thought it would be, four

rooms covering the entire third floor of the library building. The first room is dedicated to the history of Indiana County from 1750 to the present. This section looks more like a local historical society, with some Native American artifacts, including arrowheads, and nature displays. But then I came across Alex Stewart's desk from the J. M. Stewart Hardware Store, a fixture in downtown Indiana for many years. The story goes that Alex kept the hardware store open in case his son Jimmy's acting career ever fell through and he needed something "to fall back on." Don't look for the store today; it was demolished in 1969.

This native son didn't stay around too long. Born in 1908, Jimmy Stewart left town when he was fifteen to attend the Mercersburg Academy. He never lived at home again, although he visited his family often over the years. He graduated from Princeton University with a degree in architecture before pursuing his interest in theater full-time. But the town never forgot him. The Indiana University of Pennsylvania awarded him an honorary doctorate. A bronze statue with a good likeness of him graces the lawn at the county courthouse. Rouki's, a restaurant a few blocks down from the museum on Philadephia Street, is dedicated to Jimmy Stewart's movies. And now locals can point to the museum with pride.

Some people forget—or are unaware—that professionally and personally Jimmy Stewart did a whole lot more than just make an annual holiday ritual of a film. His movie career spanned fifty-seven years, from a role in *Art Trouble* (1934) to supplying a character's voice for the cartoon *An American Tail—Fievel Goes West* in 1991. In between he won an Oscar for *The Philadelphia Story* in 1940, worked with Alfred Hitchcock many times in the 1950s and 1960s, and became one of the most respected names in Hollywood. Jimmy Stewart could play comedy or drama, city man or cowboy, husband or playboy. A real anyman.

His personal life was just as eclectic. He was a pilot, a Boy Scout, a musician, a poet, a husband and father. For his work with the Boy Scouts, he was awarded the Silver Buffalo award for "Distinguished Service to Boyhood." A number of trophy cases in the museum feature his awards, such as the Hugh O'Brian Foundation Award, the AFI Award, the George Eastman Award, and the Western Heritage Award of the National Cowboy Hall of Fame for his work in *The Man Who Shot Liberty Valance*.

Jimmy Stewart never made a big deal about his military career, but he was a B-24 airplane commander in the Eighth Air Force in World War II and flew twenty combat missions over Europe. The museum has the desk and chair

149

Jimmy Stewart Museum

845 Philadelphia Street
Indiana, PA 15701
(800) 83-Jimmy or (724) 349-6112
www.jimmy.org

HOURS:

Monday–Saturday 10 A.M.–5 P.M.,
Sunday 12 P.M.–5 P.M.

DIRECTIONS:

Take the Bedford Exit from the
Pennsylvania Turnpike, and take
I-99 North to Altoona. Take Route
22 west to Ebensburg; follow the
signs to Route 422 West. Follow
422 to the Oakland
Avenue/Route 286 exit. Route
286 goes straight into Indiana.
When you reach Philadelphia
Street (the main street), the
museum building will be directly
across the street. Parking is available behind the building. The
entrance is on Ninth Street.

from his office, with both the American flag and general's flag, because Jimmy achieved the rank of brigadier general.

While the museum makes sure to cover each aspect of Jimmy's life, it naturally concentrates on his film career. An original booth from Chasen's, a favorite Hollywood restaurant, with a menu brings the glamour of old Hollywood to mind. I couldn't resist touching that red booth, even with the velvet rope in front of it. An impressive collection of both American and foreign movie posters adorns the walls.

The final section of the museum is called the Hollywood Gallery. The walls are lined with movie stills for each film he was in, and list the title, director, cast, running time, plot, and reviews. For film fans, it is a great piece of detail.

As I walked from room to room, I talked to other visitors. I met a couple from Little Valley, New York, who had driven to Indiana just to see this museum (*It's a Wonderful Life* is the wife's favorite movie). Another couple, who lives in Pittsburgh, brought friends from out of town. They told me they weren't Jimmy Stewart fans particularly, but it was a good museum and they thought their friends would enjoy it. It got me to thinking. I've been coming to this town for years to visit in-laws and yet I passed the museum by until I began writing this book. I guess I have been guilty of what I now scold people about—just not bothering because it might not be anything special. But I had been missing something. The Jimmy Stewart Museum is a wonderful retrospective on a man's life, both small-town and Hollywood.

Mattress Factory

Do you think of the art museum experience as paintings hung on immense walls in a somber and airless atmosphere? Maybe you'd be more open to the idea if the art museum had balloons and fluorescent dots and mannequins and lights? And when they handed you headphones, the recording wasn't about "the Age of Impressionism" but instead sounded something like a large army of ants? If that's the case, you're in luck. The Mattress Factory, an internationally known art museum that few Pennsylvanians are aware of, is a total sensory experience—like no other art museum I've ever been in.

Intrepid traveler Annie and I found the large, brick Mattress Factory in a residential neighborhood on Pittsburgh's North Side, the same city that gave the world Andy Warhol. In its hundred years of existence, this building has been a warehouse, a mattress factory, a candy factory, and a flood relief center. Now it sits unpretentiously among rowhomes, housing some of the most modern—postmodern? ultramodern?—art in the world.

We parked on the street and walked through the museum's

outdoor gardens into the building's lobby. The receptionist handed us some headphones and written descriptions of the exhibits for our self-guided tour. The entire exhibit was called "Visual Sound." Each artist used both visual and audio images to create a work of art, and each work had its own room. I was less familiar with many of the artists than some readers might be, but it didn't take away from my experience at all.

Each presentation is labeled with the artist's name, date of birth, and country of origin, as well as the materials used. The first one we saw, titled "Beautiful Violence," was by artist Qin Yufen (b. 1954, China). Imagine a room filled with five and three-quarter miles of barbed wire in a gnarled, comma-shaped mass. Among the wire were multicolored balloons, mostly broken, of course. About midpoint in the mass of wire was a place to step so that the barbed wire surrounded the visitor on three sides; the instructions said to think about peace. Sounds were playing but I had to read the description to know they were balloons being rubbed together and a Chinese bamboo flute being played.

I can better describe the sounds I heard while observing "Wall Blue/Wall Red" by Christine Kubisch (b. 1948, Germany). As we walked out of the elevator into the basement level, we saw blue and red electrical wires hung on the stone walls. We put on our headphones (with sixteen-channel composition!) and walked around the room. If I heard those sounds in my own cellar, I would have thought it was time to call the exterminator. But the artist had a plan; "natural sounds" came from the red side and "machine sounds" from the blue.

One exhibit we never got to see at all—at least we think so. We were walking around the museum at the same time as a group of college art students. Annie and I had just left the room with the red square of light on the wall (yes, that's all, just a red light) and walked through the next doorway. It was dark, we were on a ramp with rails on the side. The students in front of us were laughing and saying, "Can you see

Winifred Lutz, *Private Prairie*, is part of the museum's outdoor display (that's snow on the seat).

153

Mattress Factory

500 Sampsonia Way
Pittsburgh, PA 15212
(412) 231-3169
www.mattress.org

HOURS:

Tuesday–Friday 10 A.M.–5 P.M.,
Saturday 10 A.M.–7 P.M., Sunday
1 P.M.–5 P.M.

DIRECTIONS:

From the Pennsylvania Turnpike,
take the Monroeville Exit. Follow
Route 376 West to Pittsburgh.
Follow the North Side/North
Shore signs. Cross Fort Duquesne
Bridge. Stay in the left lane, following North Side/North Shore
signs. At the bottom of the ramp
(Heinz Field will be at your left)
get into right lane. At the stoplight make a right turn onto East
Allegheny. At the third light, make
a right onto North Avenue. At the
fifth light make a left onto Federal
Street. Turn left onto Jacksonia
Street and left into the parking lot
at 505 Jacksonia.

anything? I can't see anything." As we walked up the ramp
and hung on to the rail, it became darker and darker. We
could hear their chatter but we couldn't see a thing either.
We decided to stick to the lit displays and came back down
the ramp to other rooms and other experiences.

An annex to the museum with more of the same kind of
distinctive art displays is around the corner from the Mattress Factory at 1414 Monterey Street. For that house we
had to put little slippers on over our shoes because we were
walking *through* art—something we stepped on made really
crunchy sounds as we walked.

A stone shaped like an ear. Aquarium air pumps. Dirt,
with a speaker and audio. Formica and blacklights. I never
would have considered any of these an adequate medium for
art, but then I'm not an artist. "Visual Sound" was the exhibit for 2002. Each year brings something new so I can't say
what you'll see when you go.

The nearby Andy Warhol Museum gets a lot more attention in the press, but the Mattress Factory should not be
overlooked. This may be an art museum but it could never
be called "boring." Not for one minute did I think we were
wasting our time. It was fascinating and we thoroughly
enjoyed ourselves. Next time I'm in Pittsburgh, I'll probably
go back just to see what they have changed. Keep an open
mind and enjoy it.

Photo Antiquities

I wondered what I would find when I rang the bell in a doorway on East Ohio Street in Pittsburgh. This North Side neighborhood is a mix of new and old businesses. The people I saw on the street were a mix as well—residents and businesspeople, young, old, black, white—and it was noisy and bright. East Ohio Street seemed a very exciting place to be. But I wouldn't linger long. In answer to my ringing the bell, a voice came across the intercom and said, "I'll be right down."

When the door opened I met Jane Kogi, a photography graduate student. She led me up the stairs and into a world starkly different from that street scene. Here it was quiet and dimly lit. Most of the light came from the display cases housing an enormous collection of antique pictures in many forms. I was amazed at the sight and we hadn't even started the tour.

Photo Antiquities is dedicated to nineteenth-century photographic history. For the tour we began walking slowly past cases of many different types of photographs. The collection is vast and varied. Faces and more faces—mostly posed and

Yours truly Sergt. John Clem

stone serious in the fashion of the day—stared out at me. As I looked back at them, Jane explained each type of photograph or noted what was special about a particular print.

I was familiar with daguerreotypes, the earliest type of photography, which put images on copper plates. But I had never heard of ambrotypes, which are glass with a black backing. Tintypes are metal and albumen prints glass. Ivorytypes are daguerreotypes with a white backing. I have probably seen some of these others and thought they were all daguerreotypes.

Jane pointed out some calling cards, used mainly in the mid- to late 1800s. When someone called on someone else and the person wasn't home, a card would be left. I wasn't aware that some used to have photographs on them in addition to a name.

One display case had some beautiful handpainted slides. Long before the days of television, people entertained themselves with "magic lantern" shows, where a row of slides was passed through a small lantern. The light behind the slide projected the images through a lens and onto a wall or other light, smooth surface. Lantern slides were last made in the 1940s, just before television arrived. I didn't wonder, though, how people were entertained by looking at the same little pictures over and over again. A magic lantern had been passed down through my family and I was always thrilled to

see it come out for a show; occasionally my brother, Jack, still shows those same slides.

The museum preserves more than just photographs. A collection of wooden cameras sits in a room surrounded by all the proper accessories for a nineteenth-century photogra-

pher. It was not the safest of businesses. Cuff protectors kept the inevitable sparks from the flashlamps from burning the photographer's sleeves. One look at the posing rack, needed to keep subjects still for the length of time it took to make an image, and you'll understand the uncomfortable look people have in those pictures.

In another part of the museum photographic exhibits rotate from subject to subject. When I was visiting, it was the Civil War. Those dramatic battlefield pictures are not soon forgotten. Past exhibits have included women photographers, photographs of Native Americans by Edward Curtis and Karl Moon, and pictures of Pittsburgh from days past.

In our conversation, Jane and I wandered onto the subject of preservation of photographs. She told me her real love is the preservation of archival materials. We talked about the use of acid-free paper to mount pictures or whether photo albums were truly PVC-free. This visit was educational in more than one way.

This is not the Fotohut. Photo Antiquities is a long way from the Kodak Picture Maker sitting in your local drugstore waiting to scan a print and make you a new one. Children in this age of video and instant pictures probably won't understand most of the displays. But for anyone interested in images of a time past, Photo Antiquities is mesmerizing.

Photo Antiquities

531 East Ohio Street
Pittsburgh, PA 15212
(412) 231-7881
www.photoantiquities.com

HOURS:
Monday–Saturday 10 A.M.–4 P.M.

DIRECTIONS:
From Route 279 North, take Exit 13 (on right). Follow the ramp to the light. Make a left onto East Ohio Street. Photo Antiquities is two blocks on the left.

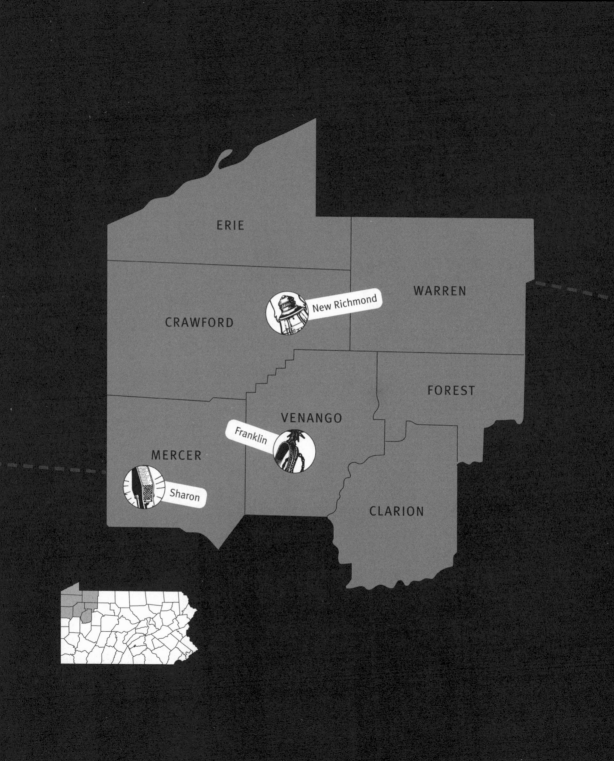

ERIE

WARREN

CRAWFORD

New Richmond

FOREST

VENANGO

Franklin

MERCER

Sharon

CLARION

HEADING FOR LAKE ERIE

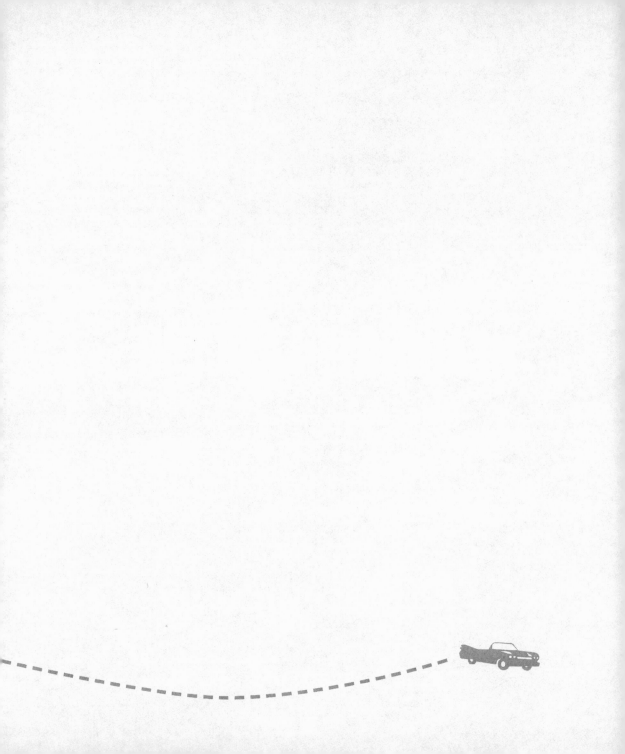

John Brown Museum

Probably few places I've visited and then described bring as strong a reaction from listeners as the tiny John Brown Museum in New Richmond. Mention of the abolitionist, famous for his unsuccessful 1859 raid on the arsenal in Harpers Ferry, West Virginia, can bring comments of scorn or admiration. Some people believe he was mentally unstable; others call him nothing less than hero.

But in 1826, when Brown came to Pennsylvania from Ohio, the raid was far in the future. Born in Connecticut and raised in Ohio by a father who preached against the evils of slavery, Brown moved to the small New Richmond settlement to build a tannery. He eventually returned to Ohio in 1835, after the deaths of his wife and two of his children, but much evidence of his stay remained.

One gray, misty, spring day my husband, Joe, and I drove east from Meadville on Route 77, looking for the historical marker that would tell us where to turn for the museum. Although its mailing address says Guys Mills, the museum is actually in New Richmond. We found it easily enough. No more than a quarter mile down John Brown Road, we pulled over in front of what remains of the tannery, a large stone foundation, with two large historical markers out front. The tannery site is now owned by the John Brown Heritage Association. We read the markers and wandered around the foundation, trying to imagine what the building must have looked like in the late 1820s.

When John Brown owned the property, it was a station on the Underground Railroad. He had a two-story log cabin and a barn with a secret hiding place for runaway slaves. Those buildings are now gone. What remains is the tannery foundation, overgrown with vegetation, and a cemetery where his first wife, Dianthe, and two of their children are buried.

As it began to rain, we decided to head toward the museum. Across the road and up some steps, at the end of a neatly mulched walkway sits the little white building that looks almost like a one-room schoolhouse. Owner Donna Coburn was waiting for us, eager to tell the story of the John Brown farm and the museum.

Donna and her husband, Gary, have owned the property since 1992, but it has been in Gary's family for much longer. His grandfather, an admirer of John Brown, purchased the land in 1947, constructed the little white building, and opened his own small John Brown museum. But it had long been closed when Donna and Gary moved in and they had no plans to revive it.

Over the years, Donna would look out her windows and see people stopping at the tannery or walking back behind her house toward the cemetery. She realized there was still a lot of interest in John Brown. To make the trek easier for visitors, she cleared a path to the gravesite. From there she began collecting items related to John Brown, and in 2001 opened her museum. In that first year 1,500 people came, some from as far away as "Nigeria, Ireland, and the Netherlands," she said proudly. "And only five of them were stinkers," she added, referring to those who didn't think John Brown deserved recognition for his antislavery efforts.

Donna has chosen to focus her museum on John Brown's

John Brown Museum

17620 John Brown Road (Route 77)
Guys Mills, PA 16327
(814) 967-2099

HOURS:

May 31–October 15, daily 10 A.M.–
6 P.M. By appointment throughout the rest of the year

DIRECTIONS:

Take Route 77 East from
Meadville ten miles. A mile after
the intersection of Route 408 is
the John Brown historical marker.
Just beyond the marker is a right
turn onto John Brown Road. The
tannery is on the right, the
museum on the left.

life in Crawford County, which brings out a side of the man people may not know. In addition to running his tannery, which employed as many as fifteen men, Brown was also a schoolteacher and the New Richmond postmaster. He is credited with bringing the first livestock to the county. And he started his own church in 1832.

The museum's glass and wood cases contain items relating to the life of John Brown or to local life at the time he lived there. On display are an ax head and pottery shards found on the farm, and a beaded purse that had belonged to Dianthe. The slave shackles on display were donated by Dr. Charles Blockson, who has written his own book on African Americans in Pennsylvania. More John Brown items can be found at the Baldwin-Reynolds House in Meadville.

Donna has also revived the John Brown Picnic, which was originally held in the early 1900s by the local John Brown Memorial Association. A poster from those early picnics, hanging on the museum wall, reads, "Music, Speaker, Food, Big Huge Celebration." The picnic is now held on the first weekend in May because Brown's birthday is May 9. Donna told us that in 2002 Civil War reenactors came to the picnic.

Harpers Ferry gives the full story of abolitionist John Brown. For John Brown the husband, father, and businessman, New Richmond is a very good place to go.

THE BEST PLACES YOU'VE NEVER SEEN

Heading for Lake Erie

Vocal Groups Hall of Fame and Museum

Only seventy-five miles from Cleveland, Ohio, is Sharon, Pennsylvania. You already know that Cleveland has the Rock 'n' Roll Hall of Fame. What you may not know is that Sharon has the Vocal Groups Hall of Fame and Museum. Cleveland may rock, but Sharon croons—sways, dips, and harmonizes, too. A little piece of glamour in a town that has seen better days.

Once vibrant, Sharon was hit hard in the mid-1980s as it lost its industries, including the largest transformer plant in the world. Enter Sharon native Tony Butala, founding member and lead singer for the Lettermen (remember "Hurt So Bad"?). Butala wanted to do something special for both his hometown and the business that made him so successful. With financial backing from local businessman James Winner, the Vocal Groups Hall of Fame and Museum opened in Sharon in 1998.

One hot July day, I drove to downtown Sharon, wondering if I'd have trouble finding the place. I didn't. Across the street from each other, the museum's two buildings, the Vocal Groups Hall of Fame and Museum and the Barbershop

To "Seger"
A Regular Fellow. - Our Pal.
Here we are, thinking aloud
are old times to gether
From
Mills Bros.
1931

Quartet Hall of Fame and Museum, stand almost as if they were in a "battle of the bands." Life-size statues of the McGuire Sisters and the Four Freshman (the latter one of Brian Wilson's big influences) stand in front of the Vocal Groups' building. The Ink Spots greet visitors at the Barbershop Hall.

Before I rave, you should know that I expected to love this place. Music is my passion. For a few days before our visit, I prepped my traveling companion and preadolescent niece, Annie, with "oldies" radio stations, explaining who was singing what, giving background on different groups, and being a virtual rock-and-roll fountain of trivia. She was patient with me.

The museum was even better than I anticipated. A video played in the lobby as we paid our entrance fee. "That's the Beach Boys," I whispered, as if it was really them and not film. The timeline that covers the wall leading into the main museum area lists vocal groups and their music over the years. I made sure to point out the large photograph of the Beatles to Annie, resisting the temptation to tell her they were the original N'Sync.

Ninety groups are featured on three floors of the museum. We saw tuxedos and sequined dresses (the Supremes!), shoes, record album covers, posters, and awards. We read about each group in a brief musical history. And, best of all, each case has a button on the side to push to hear a sample of a group's songs. It's a good thing we were alone in the museum—I sang a lot.

Centerstage on the first floor is a statue of the Mills Brothers, often called the fathers of vocal music. A push of their button brings the first strains of "Paper Doll." I hit that button more than once, just to hear those wonderful, flawless voices harmonize.

This place is a trivia buff's heaven. I didn't know that the Four Preps ("26 Miles") appeared on the *Ozzie and Harriet Show* (I thought I'd seen all the episodes!). Or that Darlene Love was one of the original members of Bob B. Soxx and the Blue Jeans (don't *make* me explain who she is—you should already know).

The vocal groups featured run from the very well known, like the Drifters, the Bee Gees, and the Fifth Dimension, to the obscure. The Three Chuckles appeared on Alan Freed's Rock-a-Rama Show. The Pixies Three, a Hanover, Pa., girl group, once opened for a very young Rolling Stones. I knew the majority of the groups, but some I didn't recognize until I heard the song, and a few I didn't know at all. I like that the museum is careful to include each decade of popular music in the museum, from the Weavers to the Backstreet Boys.

A museum highlight is the doo-wop room, decorated like an urban 1950s living room—a sofa, a few arm chairs, some end tables and lamps. As we walked into this room, off the main display area, doo-wop music began to play. Pictured out the "windows" is a streetcorner a-capella group. Chairs are available so that visitors can sit and listen a while. This is not a museum that urges you to rush through. "Why don't you staaayyy . . . just a little bit longer. . . ."

Remember, this is the Vocal Groups Hall of Fame, too. Every fall, the red carpet is rolled out—literally—for new inductees. In 2001, Mary Wilson of the Supremes attended the ceremony, where the Lennon Sisters, Gladys Knight and the Pips, the Eagles, and the Oak Ridge Boys were honored. In 2002, the fabulous Fifth Dimension was included. Now that's a diverse group!

The Barbershop Quartet building was slated to open shortly after my visit to Sharon, so I didn't get to enjoy that part of the museum. The ticket seller told me that displays for both museums are limited only by the number of musical groups they have material for, and that they are always looking for donations.

This wonderful place is not just for the trivia buff or baby boomer. At this writing, months after our visit, Annie can still sing the first strains from "Paper Doll." That makes the whole trip worthwhile.

Vocal Groups Hall of Fame and Museum

98 East State Street
Sharon, PA 16146
(724) 983-2025
www.vocalhalloffame.com

HOURS:
Thursday–Friday 4 P.M.–8 P.M., Saturday–Sunday 12 P.M.–8 P.M. Barbershop museum open on weekends only.

DIRECTIONS:
From Pittsburgh, take Route 79 North to Route 80 West to the Sharon Exit. Keep in the left lane and follow signs to East State Street in downtown Sharon.

Wild West Museum

Browsing flea markets and antique shops is a popular pastime. Dedicated collectors search everywhere for one particular item or subject matter—salt and pepper shakers or tin toys, teddy bears or Victorian jewelry. But sometimes the collection consumes the collector. Soon the house, the garage, maybe even a storage area is full of "had to haves." What is a collector to do?

Dan Hardesty is one of the lucky ones. His passion is the Wild West and he has the museum—and antiques shop—to show for it. Hardesty has been collecting Western items since he was nine years old and bought a holster. It seems only natural that he would take his passion for collecting and turn it into a business. And when his collection—the things he didn't want to resell—took up too much space among the things he wanted to sell, he opened the Wild West Museum.

My husband and I have been known to knock around antique shops for entertainment, so we looked forward to this visit. We found the museum inside a large brick building that used to be Franklin's armory. Outside are some great bronze cowboy and Indian statues, a few plaster Civil War soldiers, and a gas pump. (Okay, maybe it's not totally Wild West!)

The only real way to tell the difference between the antique shop and the museum upstairs is the velvet rope that separates them and the museum admission charge. We walked up the stairs and right past a collection of cowboy bronzes, the majority from notable Western sculptor Frederic Remington. Continuing from that point, it was paintings and posters, guns and holsters, clothing and advertisements. Cases are full, aisles are packed tight, and the rooms are not always easy to walk around in. I'm sure we missed a lot in our visit; my husband's word for it was "overwhelming."

While the general theme here is "the Wild West," the collection is unbelievably eclectic. We found historical items, from arrowheads to a cook's cabinet from a chuckwagon on the Chisolm Trail in the 1870s to a prop wig from Buffalo Bill's Wild West Show. A piece of wood is labeled as from the home of Texas gunslinger John Wesley Hardin. His story is not told in the museum but Hardin was famous for killing over thirty people. He died in 1895, shot by a man he had hired to kill

Pennsylvania cowpokes, circa 1946.

173

someone else. Supposedly, he had said he "never killed anyone who didn't need killing." I don't know if he included himself in the group that needed killing.

The Wild West played a big part in Hollywood, both on and off screen. I recognized Steve McQueen's beloved cowboy hat. We found Burt Lancaster's Winchester, Tex Ritter's gunbelt, and Pittsburgh Pirate shortstop Honus Wagner's shotgun. I never think of Sammy Davis Jr. as a Western star but he used a gun in his personal and stage appearances and it's in the museum.

The collection sometimes drifts into other subjects. A stuffed wolf, Civil War guns, Nazi items, even a newspaper clipping on the 1969 moon walk—the "final frontier," of course. But it is mainly the West, past and present.

This museum is not just "collectibles"—things made for the collector market that can be bought new today—passed off as historical items. A lot of the pieces, such as Geronimo's burial shroud, have certificates of authenticity. On the other hand, a typed note on a photograph of Two Guns White Calf of the Blackfeet tribe says he posed for the buffalo nickel. I did a little research and found that the identities of the models for the five-cent piece have been debated since it came into circulation. The artist who designed the engraving claims that Two Guns was not among those chosen.

The road to one museum has often led me to another I didn't know about. One museum owner recommended I visit Flip Side Collectors Mall in Hermitage, Pa., if I was down that way. Flip Side is a record and antique shop, but it also has a lot of rock'n'roll memorabilia on display. Most of the items—including one of Elvis's saddles, which was there during my visit to the Flip Side—are for sale. On another trip I stumbled across an antique shop/museum on Route 30 between Breezewood and Bedford. Old Tyme Antiques has one museum room full of dazzling carnival glass and spittoons—no labels or descriptions, just glass and spittoons.

Dan warns that potential Wild West Museum visitors should call first. If he has a good auction to go to, he may just "close up and leave." During our conversation he talked about retiring, but then moved on to show me "just one more thing." His enthusiasm is infectious. I asked him, "You're never going to stop collecting, are you?"

He smiled widely and shook his head. "No." Not a bad thing when you can put your passion and your work together, is it?

Wild West Museum

1280 Franklin Avenue
Franklin, PA 16323
(814) 432-8577

HOURS:
Monday–Saturday 10 A.M.–5 P.M.,
Sunday 12 P.M.–5 P.M.

DIRECTIONS:
From the east, driving on I-80, take Route 322 west at Clarion. Follow 322 to Routes 8/62 in Franklin. Turn right on 13th Street and right again on Franklin (right before the bridge crossing the river). The museum is in the antique shop in the old armory. *From the west,* driving on I-80, take the exit for Route 8. Go north on Route 8; it will merge with Route 62 and run right through downtown Franklin. Turn left on 13th Street and right on Franklin (right before the bridge crossing the river). The museum is in the antique shop in the old armory.

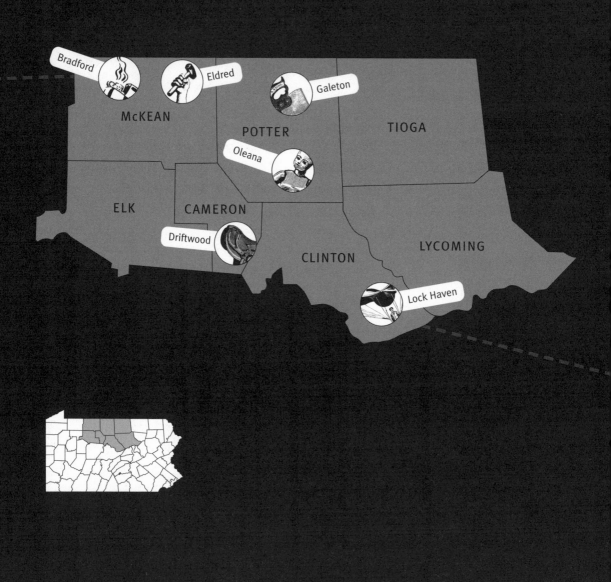

Bradford

Eldred

Galeton

McKEAN

POTTER

TIOGA

Oleana

ELK

CAMERON

Driftwood

CLINTON

LYCOMING

Lock Haven

TOP OF THE WORLD

Eldred World War II Museum

You might think Eldred an unlikely place for a museum dedicated to World War II. This tiny town, dwarfed even by neighboring Bradford, sits quietly near the New York border. Its closest highway is the scenic, meandering Route 6. So why put a war museum in such a peaceful place? Because Eldred, Pa., has a history as a weapons manufacturer.

In 1939 the war in Europe was creeping closer to England. The British knew they needed to prepare for it and hired American George Rodebush to find U.S. land for a munitions plant for the Royal Air Force. Rodebush chose Eldred. Construction on a sixty-two-building National Munitions Company plant began in 1940 and, when it was completed, workers there made mortar shells. After Pearl Harbor, another plant was constructed in Eldred to make incendiary bombs for use by U.S. forces.

Like many museum tours I've made, this one starts with a video. This film on the history of the plants and the war gives visitors a good idea of what life was like in war-time Eldred and how dangerous plant work could be. Workers handled explosive materials and many precautions had to be taken.

the Women Behind the Front Lines...

Each plant building even had an escape chute in case of an accident. In all, the Eldred plants of the 1940s produced 8 million bombs, mortar shells, and fuses. Despite their best efforts, though, fewer than half those munitions made it overseas—too many Nazi patrols in the Atlantic.

I visited Eldred with my husband, Joe, whose father was a veteran of World War II. After the video, we wandered through the two floors and many rooms of the museum. Museum curator Susan Black told me that the collection keeps expanding because veterans are constantly donating their belongings. Many items on display are similar to what my father-in-law brought home from Europe—canteens, handbooks, sewing kits, shaving kits, compasses, stationery sets, Nazi flags, and red-lens gunnery glasses. The colorful sandals, cups, and painted shells came from Pacific veterans.

The museum displays more than GI-issue personal property, however. One diorama illustrates the problems of the French hedgerows in the Battle of the Bulge; another depicts the Battle of Midway. Those who did not see battle are memorialized as well, with reminders of the death camps and civilians caught in the midst of fighting.

Weapons don't just fire ammo. We saw the once "top secret" Norden bombsight, a Mark 18 gunsight, and the

"Porto-Clinic: The Complete Portable Psychophysical Driver Testing Unit." The Porto-Clinic was used to test pilots' eye-hand coordination and even had a role, along with the Norden bombsight, in the wartime movie *Bombadier.*

Not all exhibits are permanent; some rotate. When we visited, they were preparing a display of Jeeps and other vehicles used in wartime. The reference library is gaining its own reputation. When Walter Cronkite was collecting letters for his book on World War II, he turned to the Eldred museum for help obtaining Russian correspondence.

Some displays are geared toward children, to try to get them to understand something about what the war was like. They can try on uniforms, learn about scrap drives, or how to identify "the enemy." During my visit a boy played constantly with the remote-control tank in a mountain obstacle course. His mother couldn't pull him away.

In addition to its subject matter, what draws me to this museum is its inclusiveness. It's not just soldiers and guns. It's the homefront, it's the munitions workers, it's male and female, young and old. Everyone pitched in, everyone played a role in that war, everyone made sacrifices. And they are all recognized for their efforts.

Eldred World War II Museum

201 Main Street
Eldred, PA 16731
(814) 225-2220
www.eldredwwiimuseum.org

HOURS:

Tuesday, Thursday, and Saturday
10 A.M.–4 P.M.; Sunday 1 P.M.–4 P.M.
Other hours by appointment.

DIRECTIONS:

From Route 6, go north on Route
155 to Route 446. Route 446 is
Eldred's main street; the museum
is on the left.

If you watch the History Channel, you know the history of the war. But nothing can compare with seeing real letters from a soldier, looking at a shaving kit and trying to imagine how close that shave was in a war zone, or wondering what that old KA-Bar must have tasted like. Many World War II veterans have visited the museum, but everyone else should, too. It's a part of all of us.

Ole Bull Museum

A family reunion led me to this remote part of Pennsylvania one summer day. When my cousins Ed and Jerry heard I was exploring little museums in Pennsylvania, they laughed as they told me to see the Ole Bull Museum. I'm sure they'll be surprised to know I went. And it turned out to be a visit I'll never forget.

When I drove north on Route 44, through towns like Haneyville and Carter Camp, I honestly wondered where I was headed. I'd never been in this part of the state and it appears that's the case for a lot of people. Potter County is mountainous and not very populated. But it's easy to see from the beautiful scenery why Norwegian violinist Ole Bull was drawn here in the mid-1800s.

Ole Bull is not exactly a household name. With 800 Norwegian immigrants, he started a colony in Potter County in 1852. He began by building a castle, but within three years the colony had disbanded and the castle was left unfinished. The hard life they faced in the Pennsylvania mountains was too much, and most of them moved west toward other Scandinavian settlements. The complete story of the settlement,

as well as remnants of the castle, can be found just down the road at Ole Bull State Park (see also http://www.dcnr.state.pa.us/state-parks/parks/ole.htm).

Continuing north past Carter Camp, I rounded a curve and saw small red buildings on the left side of the road above me on the hill. I pulled the car to the side and parked. As I approached the steps leading toward this little colony, I heard dogs barking, and a petite, elderly woman came out.

From the start, I knew this was no run-of-the-mill roadside museum. No other owner I visited had been in costume, but Inez greeted me in full bright-red Norwegian dress and introduced herself as the great-grandniece of Ole Bull. Inez invited me to take as many pictures as I wished as we walked among the buildings. She was rather hard of hearing, so mostly I just listened. But she was full of stories to tell.

An only child, Inez was very close to her mother, Aurora. After they lost Inez's father in World

War II, Inez told me, to ease her mother's grief "I built these little buildings as wedding anniversary gifts to my mother." Inez said she bought the land the museum stands on in 1946 because it was part of Ole Bull's original holdings. Over the years she added to the property, ending up with ten small buildings.

Each structure has its own theme. Some buildings we entered and walked around in. For those that were too small, she would just throw open the doors and proudly explain the contents. My favorite was the stave church with, as Inez says, "enough room for one person and one Bible." Actually it's big enough for two people and a Bible. Modeled after a full-size church in Telemark, Norway, the little chapel has an altar in the shape of a sheaf of wheat and a cross made by one of Inez's many friends. On the wall is a photo of the statue of Ole Bull that stands in Loring Park, Minneapolis.

I recognized the *stabbur hus,* a rounded-roof building with a much larger top half than bottom. Inez told me that's where families in Norway stored their meat, their money, and their women and children if safety was a problem.

A tiny building at the end of the row is dedicated to Finn Ronne, a Norwegian who gained fame when he rescued Admiral Richard Byrd in the Antarctic. On display are the flag that flew over Antarctica, a *Look* magazine featuring the rescue, and Ronne's skis and boots, which were a gift to Inez from Ronne's wife.

Two of the buildings in particular hold items that were dear to Inez's mother, Aurora Stewart Bull, who died in 1976. "The Doll's House" (yes, it's an Ibsen reference) contains Aurora's doll collection. The last building on the tour is the

OPPOSITE: Inez Bull and her "one person, one Bible" chapel

"Mother Goose Bed and Breakfast," which contains children's toys and radio memorabilia. Inez said her mother was the original "Mother Goose Girl" for a children's radio program in New York.

Inez likes to commemorate people and places she respects. A plaque on a rock next to one building is dedicated to conservationist Maurice Goddard, whom she calls "a saint." A tree nearby has a sign that says "planted by Inez Bull on 8/1/1952 with soil from Ole Bull's home." A photograph shows King Harald V of Norway decorating Inez with the St. Olaf medal on June 2, 1999.

Inez has had a colorful career. She sang at Carnegie Hall and toured with violinist Vladimir Padiva for seventeen years—her press clippings adorn the walls in the main museum building. She was a music teacher in New Jersey. She has also orchestrated the Ole Bull Music Festival in Potter County for fifty years. A stack of books that Inez has written on childhood education sits on a table; some are for sale. In the winter she lives in New Jersey, but every June she returns to Pennsylvania with a truckload of items for the Ole Bull Museum.

From her musical career to the books to the connections to Norway to Ole Bull—it was a lot to take in on one visit. I still don't believe I grasped it all. At the time, I wondered if I'd just come across a Potter County Brigadoon. Since I visited alone, I had no one with whom to compare my impressions. The name "Oleana" doesn't even appear on the state map—the mailing address is Galeton. But I knew I had been in this little place and I wanted to find out more about it.

When I returned home, I searched for Inez Bull's name on the Internet. On a Potter County bulletin board I found a note from Beth in Williamsport. She had stopped at the Ole Bull Museum on a whim the year before. She felt the same way I did—it's an unforgettable experience. You may discover some disputes about Inez's claims, but I chose to lay them aside and take everything as I saw it. She was a warm, welcoming person and it was a fascinating visit.

I can't guarantee the museum will be open if you go. Definitely call first. If you're going to take the trek out to Ole Bull, make sure you have a full tank of gas. I ran out on the way home, at the edge of state game lands north of Snow Shoe. But with the kindness of strangers, I was soon on my way again. I'll never forget my rescuers—or Inez Bull.

Ole Bull Museum

South Cherry Springs Road
Route 144
Galeton, PA 16922
(814) 435-2619

free ☺

HOURS:

Mid-June–September 15, daily
2 P.M.–8 P.M. Call ahead.

DIRECTIONS:

From Galeton on Route 6, go south on Route 144. At the Route 44 intersection at Carter Camp, turn right. Ole Bull is on the left, two miles north of Carter Camp.

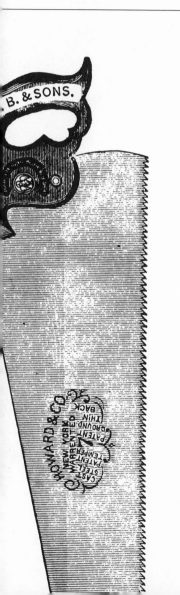

Pennsylvania Lumber Museum

So maybe the thought of a "lumber museum" puts you to sleep. Maybe you think wood is just something for the fireplace. But there's more to lumber than sawing logs. This museum, owned by the Pennsylvania Historical and Museum Commission, thoroughly illustrates the history of the lumber industry in Pennsylvania with displays, demonstrations, and—of course—the annual Bark Peelers' Convention.

Lumber has always been a major contributor to Pennsylvania's economy. According to the museum's official history, over 90 percent of Pennsylvania was wooded when William Penn arrived. And a mere one hundred years ago Pennsylvania was still supplying a significant amount of the white pine and hemlock lumber used throughout the United States. So it is only natural that the state would have a lumber museum.

The rustic wooden main building, along Route 6 between Galeton and Coudersport, actually contains two museums. One large room focuses on logging (getting logs from forest to market). A diorama in the center of the room illustrates the entire logging process, from cutting a tree to rafting the logs down the river, as they did in the days before trucks.

Real lumberjack tools and photographs aid in explaining the procedure.

As I was staring at the massive axes, saws, and other tools, all I could think was how strong lumberjacks had to be in the days before machines. No wonder they had a reputation for being tough. Timbering was dangerous and very hard work. Many "woodhicks," as the workers were known, died on the job. With so many improvements in safety and mechanics, it's a different job today. The days of the woodhick are gone, but visitors get a good idea of what life was like for them.

The other room—much to my surprise—is dedicated to the Civilian Conservation Corps (CCC). Although the CCC's handiwork appears all over the country, the story of the men who lived and worked in the CCC camps is not very well known to younger generations. (For a complete history of the CCC, visit www.cccalumni.org.) During the Depression, the U.S. government created the CCC to

put unemployed young men to work building roads, planting trees, stringing telephone lines. The men of the CCC handled whatever public-works task that was put before them. Enrollment lasted a minimum of six months, giving the men a chance to learn some skills and earn $30 a month, of which $25 was automatically sent back to the worker's family.

A CCC cabin has been moved onto the Lumber Museum's property and is open to visitors. Seeing the spare conditions—with fireplaces and wooden bunkbeds—reminded me of the soldiers' cabins at Valley Forge Park. The CCC workers had a few more luxuries, with things like sinks and easier access to firewood, than the soldiers in 1776 but it was still not easy living. Evidence of the CCC is closer to state residents than you might be aware. Many state parks contain cabins built by the CCC. If you're near Promised Land State Park in Pike County (http://www.dcnr.state.pa.us/stateparks/parks/p-land.htm), stop by their little museum dedicated to the CCC and say hello to the stuffed black bear.

The Bark Peelers' Convention is held on the first weekend in July. Attractions include demonstrations of antique engines, log skidding (for all you non-woodhicks, that means moving logs), hewing, and blacksmithing. Attendees can also participate in tobacco-spitting, fiddling, and greased-pole contests. Maybe I'll make it next year—I've always wanted to try my hand (or feet?) at birling.

Over my museum visits I was surprised at times to learn which collections are rigged with alarms. One might think that a lumber museum would have no concerns about light-fingered visitors—what could you do, skid a log? But let this be a lesson: My cousin Ed (with no previous rap sheet) once saw a plate in a Lumber Museum display similar to one he has at home. Curious about the plate's origins, and after looking around to see if he was being watched, he stepped over the rope to examine the plate more closely. As he tells it, before he knew what was happening, he was handcuffed and questioned (fortunately they believed his explanation and let him go; his record is still clean). The lesson here is "Just ask." The folks at all the Pennsylvania small museums will be happy to answer your questions.

This is a larger museum than most I visited, but a visitor can choose how much to see and still have it be a worthwhile visit. Children will enjoy the outdoor exhibits as much as the indoor, including a sawmill, blacksmith shop, the woodhicks' mess hall and bunks, loader shed, horse barn, and more. You may want to call ahead to see what demonstrations will be taking place during your visit. Timmmm-berrrrr!

Pennsylvania Lumber Museum

5660 U.S. 6 West
P.O. Box K
Galeton, PA 16922
(814) 435-2652
www.lumbermuseum.org

HOURS:
April–November, daily, 9:00 A.M.–5:00 P.M., except Columbus Day, Veterans Day, Thanksgiving Day, and the day after Thanksgiving. December–March, open by chance or by appointment

DIRECTIONS:
The Lumber Museum is on Route 6 just west of Galeton.

Piper Aviation Museum

"Flying a Piper Cub is like flying a kite." That's what my tour guide said to me when I visited the Piper Aviation Museum. I pictured myself holding onto the strings and watching that Cub crash like so many kites before it. Then he said, "Very simple." I wasn't convinced. I still think I'll leave the piloting to the pilots and stick to crashing kites.

My lack of aviation skills, though, didn't mean I found the Piper Aviation Museum a drag. In fact, it was far more a lift. Inside the large brick structure that used to be Piper's engineering building, I paid my admission and glanced through the guest book. In addition to names and addresses, they ask if the visitor is a pilot. On the open page, I counted four pilots and nine nonpilots, including one optimist who wrote "not yet."

Another purely Pennsylvania operation, Piper Aviation came from the mind and energy of a Bradford, Pa., native. Committed to the idea of "aviation for the common man," William Piper Sr. started his business in Bradford in partnership with C. Gubert Taylor in 1931. Their first plane was the "Taylor Chummy." In 1937 Piper bought Taylor out, the factory burned to the ground, and Piper moved to Lock Haven. Over the next 47 years the Piper Aviation Company made 73,637 planes.

My tour guide, Russ Nelson, is a pilot and one of the museum volunteers. He can probably fly kites, too. But I was there to see planes and plane stuff so that's what we did. The ground floor of the museum holds life-sized planes.

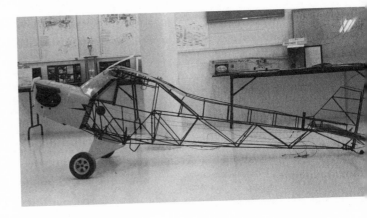

Model frame of a Piper J-3 Cub.

The most familiar is the Piper J-3 Cub, with its unmistakable yellow color. In the 1970s the Piper Aztec "was their Cadillac," Russ said, "very fine, very sophisticated." It had tricycle landing gear, two engines, and could seat four people. Nice features for a personal aircraft.

These cheerful little planes don't bring wartime to mind, but during World War II Piper wanted to help in the conflict. With some support from General Dwight Eisenhower, who saw the plane's value, Piper was awarded a contract for 1,500 planes. The Piper L-4 was used for reconnaissance, artillery spotting, and ambulance service. The Seabees even built a runway on aircraft carriers specifically designed for Piper Cubs.

In 1947 flight instructors Clifford Evans and George Truman took two PA-12 Super Cruisers around the world. It may not seem like so much now, with people traversing the world in a balloon, but this was the first time a light plane had circumnavigated the globe. One of the pair, "The City of Washington," can be found in the Smithsonian. After 1,500

Piper Aviation Museum

One Piper Way
Lock Haven, PA 17745
(570) 748-8283
www.pipermuseum.com

HOURS:
Monday–Friday 9 A.M.–4 P.M.,
Saturday 10 A.M.–4 P.M., Sunday
12 P.M.–4 P.M.

DIRECTIONS:
From I-80, take Route 150 North
and follow the signs to the airport.

hours of restoration work "from the ground up," the other plane, "The City of the Angels," is one of the Piper Museum's showpieces.

After seeing the planes, Russ and I walked upstairs past some trainers for instrument flying and other equipment before heading to the large room with the history and photographs. Small plane enthusiasts could probably spend hours in this section, but children will be more interested in the actual planes. Some displays honor pilots through the years, like Alma Heflin. She was Piper's public relations director in the 1930s and always flew "dressed to the nines." I liked the quote from pilot recordbreaker Max Conrad: "There are old pilots and there are bold pilots, but there are no old, bold pilots." Point taken.

I look forward to the day when I can return to the museum and try out the Piper Tomahawk II flight simulator. At my visit, restoration was half finished, but now it's complete. Visitors can now "fly" the plane with a video screen showing how they're doing (no strings!).

The Piper Company has gone through hard times. Tropical Storm Agnes destroyed $22 million of its planes in 1972. After a hostile takeover, the company moved out of the family's hands and left Lock Haven for Florida in 1985. These days the Piper Company makes corporate jets like the Cheyenne, a far cry from that canary yellow Cub.

With the help of local businesses and many ex-employees, though, the museum is going strong. The planes in the museum can be seen all year long, but if you hanker for more, go in June for the Piper fly-in when as many as 500 planes come home to roost.

Tom Mix Birthplace and Museum

When I headed out for the Tom Mix Birthplace and Museum, I figured I'd be stepping back in time. Maybe some friendly cowpoke would greet me with "Howdy, little lady" and tip his dusty hat. Or at least "Mornin', ma'am," as he swung up on his horse and rode off to attend to his chores.

Well, I was partly right. I did go back in time. But not where I expected.

To get to the Tom Mix Birthplace, I drove about four miles off Route 555, on both paved and gravel roads, through dense woods at times, following a small car and roughly painted signs the entire way. I wasn't surprised when the small car pulled into the Tom Mix driveway ahead of me; there wasn't much else out there.

The two men entered the rustic front-office/gift shop for the Tom Mix Birthplace and Museum just before me. When I stepped through the doorway, I was immediately greeted by the owner, Ray Flaugh, with "You know what we follow around here? Genesis 3:16! Do you know what that is?"

My first thought: "Was that the first album after Phil Collins left the band?" But wisely I just shook my head. Ray

"IT WAS SAID THAT **TOM MIX COULD RIDE ANYTHING** that walked."

—promotional copy for Tom Mix Museum

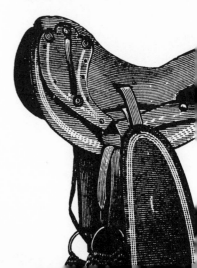

proudly said, "That's the one where the man's master over the woman! What do you think of that?"

Knowing that I was unprepared for a theological debate, I just told Ray that I was sure the Bible had been interpreted in many different ways over the years. The two men who had walked in just before me laughed. And my answer was enough to make Ray turn to what he knows best—Tom Mix.

Tom Mix—for the uninitiated—was the first cowboy of the silver screen. Before Gene Autry and Roy Rogers, there was Tom Mix and his trusty steed, Tony (and later Tony Jr.). Many a present-day grandfather was a Ralston Straight Shooter in the 1930s, including the two men with whom I toured the museum.

Born in 1880 in what was then Mix Run, Pennsylvania, Tom didn't hang around town long. His family moseyed on over to DuBois when he was four; his father changed jobs. It was probably better they left, because in the late 1880s Cameron County was a pretty rough place. Ray will be more than happy to tell you the story of Mix's uncles, Warren "Tricky" Mix and Newton Mix (pay attention—it involves murder and revenge).

Despite these rough beginnings and a fourth-grade education, Tom Mix triumphed. After a stint in the Army, Mix started performing in Wild West shows, eventually settling into a successful film career. Legions of fans lined up at moviehouses to watch Tom Mix fight the bad guys on Saturday afternoons. At home they listened faithfully to his radio show, saving Ralston boxtops to order the latest Tom Mix adventure comic.

Site of the biggest crime ever to hit Cameron County.

Many big names in Hollywood worked with Tom Mix before they hit it big. John Wayne once worked as his prop man, and Mickey Rooney's first picture was with Tom Mix. Even Ronald Reagan knew Mix; when the birthplace was being restored, Reagan sent a donation. (Ray proudly showed me a photocopy of the check.)

Mix made over 350 movies and did all his own stunts because he believed that's what people were paying to see. But real life isn't the movies: Tom Mix died in October 1940 in a car accident. He was racing a friend (who was in an airplane) in Florence, Arizona, when his car rolled over.

Ray and his wife, Eva, have had the museum for nearly twenty years. The tour includes watching a Philadelphia news magazine video about the museum, filmed in the early 1990s, and a tour of the outbuildings. But wandering around the museum itself is far more interesting. Ray Flaugh has a vast collection of Mix memorabilia—comic books, games, Ralston cereal ads, pocket knives. My favorite was the map

Tom Mix Birthplace and Museum

R.D. 1, Box 54
Driftwood, PA 15832
(814) 546-2044 or 2628

HOURS:

Daily 10 A.M.–4 P.M. from mid-April to the end of September.

DIRECTIONS:

Take Route 120 from Lock Haven or Emporium to Driftwood and follow the well-placed signs. You'll be on back roads (some gravel) for much of the way from Driftwood.

made of Mix's body, showing his injuries over the years, which one of my tour companions clearly remembered receiving in the mail.

While the foundation is still visible on the grounds, the Mix family's house has been gone for years. But people still come from all over the world to see where Tom Mix was born. I met Ralston Straight Shooter Curt Shaw of Tidioute, Pennsylvania, on his second visit to the museum. If we had come a week later, we would have been in time for the annual Tom Mix Roundup (the third week in July). Ray told me they have a full weekend of activities during the Roundup, including dances with fiddle music, a Wild West kissing contest, and picture-taking with a Tom Mix look-alike.

This museum also offers an opportunity for visitors like no other place I visited. For $10 you can own a one-inch-square lot of real estate from the Tom Mix Birthplace, with a signed certificate stating that you own it. The Flaughs have a grid drawn to show buyers the exact location of their piece. Ronald Reagan owns a piece (and has a marker to that effect), as does Willie Nelson, who visited several years ago.

For Ralston Straight Shooters, this place is a must-see. Radio and film buffs will enjoy it, too. For the rest of us—whether city slicker or tenderfoot—it's still fun.

Zippo Case Museum

Glitz! Glamour! Zippo lighters! Huh? Does that seem possible? Guaranteed, this museum will surprise—even dazzle—you. The Zippo Visitors Center claims to be the "most visited museum in northern Pennsylvania," which I don't doubt based on the crowds I saw one summer afternoon. And why not? It's bright, it's interesting, and it will entertain children of all ages.

I was treated to the Zippo tour as part of a day at a family reunion. We're not a group of smokers by any means, but we found a lot to like in our visit. You can't miss the Visitors Center off Route 219, with its forty-foot lighter, complete with neon flame, above the entrance. Once we were inside, the museum entrance, with its flashing lights, immediately beckoned us into a dark walkway and the beginning of the Zippo tour.

First stop, a timeline for world history covering an entire wall, combined with that of the Zippo and Case companies, from 1784 to 1997. (Case is a knife manufacturer and, since 1993, a subsidiary of Zippo.) Bet you can find a lot you don't know; my favorite trivia fact was that in 1931 Bradford's

"days as 'Little Chicago' were over." The grownups stopped to read the timeline. The children ran on ahead.

A little company history: in 1931, just as Bradford was cleaning up its act and losing its gangster identity, George Blaisdell ran into a friend on the porch of the Bradford Country Club. Smokers have always had difficulty lighting up in a breeze. Blaisdell noticed that his friend's lighter worked under any conditions. He obtained the U.S. distribution rights for this marvelous Austrian lighter, redesigned the case and windproof chimney, and the Zippo Windproof Lighter was born. The all-important striking wheel was added in 1946.

Next we came to an enormous seven-by-eleven–foot American flag made of 3,393 Zippo lighters, which was completed in 2000. It's a marvel to look at; I had no clue that there were so many different designs. Zippo obviously kept a close eye on popular culture. The company made lighters to note historical events, to honor stars, even to appeal to both genders. Cars, scenic places, famous people, companies—it seems they didn't miss a thing.

Zippo is proud to say that their lighters have been a part of every war since World War II. Soldiers rely on them for more than just smoking. Zippos can start campfires or be used for light. Some soldiers expressed a more creative side with their Zippos; they used them for "trench art." On one lighter a soldier's feelings about his time overseas are carved: "If I had a farm in Vietnam and a home in hell, I'd sell my farm and go home."

Since it was Saturday we couldn't witness the Famous Zippo Repair Clinic in operation, but a big glass window let us see the tables and repair tools used to repair lighters. Zippo enthusiasts can mail their lighters to Zippo to have them fixed—over 14 million have been repaired so far, all at no charge.

In the Hollywood section, we saw that Zippo lighters have been featured in over 800 movie roles. (I can't imagine who counted them up.) But Zippos did so much more than just light a cigarette in a romantic scene or illuminate a private detective's face in the shadows. In *Die Hard* Bruce Willis used a Zippo so he could see in an airshaft and in *Die Harder* he used one to blow up a plane when the bad guys were escaping. As the ad says, "Why zip zip zip when one zip does it!"

The children in our group had run up ahead to ZAC (short for Zippo and Case), the seven-foot kinetic ball machine. It features both a lighter and a knife that open and close, and a Zippo lighter flame. The kids were transfixed, watching billiard balls run down the chutes from piece to piece, roll, fall, and go up to start again. I paused to play some video trivia games until everyone was ready to go.

If you can't make it to Bradford anytime soon, try Zippo's website (www.zippo.com) for a virtual tour of the museum. It doesn't take the place of the original, but it gives a very clear picture of what is included. But if you're up that way, go ahead and stop.

Zippo Case Museum

1932 Zippo Drive
Bradford, PA 16701
(888) 442-1932
www.zippo.com

HOURS:

Monday–Saturday 9 A.M.–5 P.M.,
Sunday 12 P.M.–4 P.M.

DIRECTIONS:

Take the Zippo exit from the Route 219 Expressway in Bradford.

Acknowledgments

Now I know why authors always say they couldn't have written their book without help. Many, many people had a voice in this book, letting me know what they liked as well as when I was headed in the wrong direction.

First, I must thank all the small museum curators, guides, and volunteers I met. They each took time—often hours—to show me their museum, talk to me about it, and answer my never-ending questions, even if it was after closing time on the day before a holiday and they were on standby pumpkin-pie duty. Their enthusiasm was infectious and I always left knowing more than when I arrived.

My extended family and many friends have been consistently supportive and full of ideas. I'm sorry I can't name them all here, but I thank each one of them for their patience and advice. In the end, it became a game of "stump the author": someone would say, "Have you heard of . . . ?" A "Yes" answer always brought disappointment but kept them looking for more. Some of these places never would have been found without their help.

A number of people visited the museums with me, gave me stories about their own visits, or read parts of the manuscript and gave me feedback. For that I thank Joyce Black, Annie Boyd, Candace Boyd, Miriam Close Boyd, Leigh Cohen and David Burke, Caitlin Haywood Conroy, Ed Pecht, and all my "Writing Your Life Story" students.

I want to thank Penn State Press for their enthusiastic

acceptance of this book. I've been an editor and a writer for many years, but I still didn't realize what kind of beast I was tackling. Editor Gloria Kury, Tim Holsopple, and the rest of the staff never failed to encourage my efforts.

Rich Engel took a number of the photographs for this book; his eye for detail is evident. I don't know how he can make things look so good, but he does. Many people at the various museums assisted me in collecting some of the other pictures: Jeanette A'psis at the Insectarium; Bruce Bazelon at the Pennsylvania Historical and Museum Commission; Susan Black at the Eldred World War II Museum; Donna Coburn at the John Brown Museum; Jack Cohen at the Mummers Museum; Melanie Doorly at Yuengling; Judi Laubach at Bill's Old Bike Barn; the Reverend Jeffrey Leath at Mother Bethel A.M.E. Church; Rob Leonard at the Wharton Esherick Studio; Steve Mahon at Zippo; Ed Mazeika at Apollo Designs; Ed Reis at the George Westinghouse Museum; Tracy Rogers at the Vocal Groups Hall of Fame and Museum; Pam Seighman at the Coal and Coke Heritage Center; Thomas Thompson at the Christian Sanderson Museum; Barbara Williams at the Shoe Museum; and Scott Yoss at Photo Antiquities.

I'd like to thank the people who filled my gas tank when I ran out, let me sleep on their couches, and listened to me rave about my latest find even when they were tired of hearing about it. You know who you are. I also want to thank Steve Forbert; without his music to keep me company, it would have been a much longer road.

In the end, this book exists only because of two very important people in my life. The first is my husband, Joe

Acknowledgments

Pizarchik. Familiar with my skills at procrastination, he was always able to remind me that I had to complete the book, prodding me gently to keep going, encouraging me when it seemed I would never finish. He knows I appreciate everything he did.

And, I can never thank Patty Mitchell enough. This book was her idea. She read early drafts and copyedited the final manuscript. Most important, she has been my dear friend for a very long time and we've covered many, many miles together. We're a long way from cruising Sinking Valley, Mitch, but, hey, at least we're still on the road.

Because these museums are mentioned in the book, I list them here. I have visited some but not all of them.

◉ **Appendix**

Other Small Museums Mentioned

African-American Historical and Cultural Museum
701 Arch Street
Philadelphia, PA 19106-1557
(215) 574-0380
www.aampmuseum.org

Allegheny Portage Railroad Museum
110 Federal Park Road
Gallitzin, PA 16641
(814) 886-6150
www.nps.gov/alpo/index.htm

Antique Auto Club of America Museum
(completion of new facilities set for 2003)
115 Museum Drive
Hershey, PA 17033
(717) 566-7100
www.aacamuseum.org

Andy Warhol Museum
117 Sandusky Street
Pittsburgh, PA 15212-5890
(412) 237-8300
www.warhol.org

Baldwin-Reynolds House Museum
639 Terrace St.
Meadville, PA 16335
(814) 333-9882

Central Pennsylvania African-American Museum
119 N. Tenth Street
Reading, PA 19601
(610) 371-8713

Electric City Trolley Museum
Cliff Street, at Steamtown National Historic Site
Scranton, PA 18503
(570) 963-6590
www.ectma.org/museum.html

**Flip Side Collectors' Mall
(Antique Mall)**
940 N. Hermitage Road
Hermitage, PA 16148
(724) 342-0824
www.flipmall.com

Hershey Museum
170 W. Hersheypark Drive
Hershey, PA 17033
(717) 534-3439
www.hersheymuseum.org

Jerry's Classic Cars
394 S. Centre Street
Pottsville, PA 17901
(570) 628-2266 or (888) 802-6605
www.jerrysmuseum.com

**Johnstown Flood National
Memorial**
733 Lake Road
South Fork, PA 15956
(814) 495-4643
www.nps.gov/jofl/

Lackawanna Coal Mine
McDade Park
Scranton, PA 18504
(570) 963-6463 or (800) 238-7245
www.lackawannacounty.org

Moravian Archives Museum
8 Church Street
Lititz, PA 17543
(717) 626-8515

Museum of Anthracite Mining
Pine and 17th Streets
Ashland, PA 17921
(717) 875-4708
www.ashlandpa.org/attractions/
museum.htm

National Watch and Clock Museum
514 Poplar Street
Columbia, PA 17152
(717) 684-8261
www.nawcc.org

Pennsylvania Trolley Museum
1 Museum Road
Washington, PA 15301
(724) 228-9256
www.pa-trolley.org

Pioneer Tunnel Coal Mine
19th and Oak Streets
Ashland, PA 17921
(570) 875-3850
www.ashlandpa.org/attractions/pioneer.htm

Railroaders Memorial Museum
1300 Ninth Avenue
Altoona, PA 16602
(814) 946-0834
www.railroadcity.com

Reading Railroad Museum
Canal and Wall Streets
Leesport, PA 19533
(610) 926-0253
www.readingrailroad.org

Seldom Seen Coal Mine
P.O. Box 83
Patton, PA 16668
(814) 247-6305 or 674-8939
www.seldomseenmine.com

**Wilbur Candy Americana
Museum and Store**
48 N. Broad St.
Lititz, PA 17543
(717) 626-3249
www.wilburbuds.com

Windber Coal Heritage Center
501 15th St.
Windber, PA 15963
(814) 467-6680

Bill's Old Bike Barn: 4 Judi Laubach. **5** Therese Boyd.

Bob Hoffman Weightlifting Hall of Fame and Museum: 78 From John D. Fair, *Muscletown USA: Bob Hoffman and the Manly Culture of York Barbell* (University Park: Penn State Press, 1999), 41; illustration by Joe Miller. **79** Therese Boyd.

Boyertown Museum of Historical Vehicles: 30, 33 Rich Engel/Image Productions.

Christian Sanderson Museum: 35, 37, 38 Courtesy Christian Sanderson Museum.

Coal and Coke Heritage Center: 139, 140 Courtesy Coal and Coke Heritage Center.

Eldred World War II Museum: 180 Tony Sanfilippo. **181** From the collection of Tony and Mary Pizarchik. **182** Tony Sanfilippo.

First National Bank Museum: 82 Courtesy First National Bank Museum.

Gardners Candies: 106 Therese Boyd. **107** Patricia A. Mitchell.

George Westinghouse Museum: 143, 144 Courtesy George Westinghouse Museum.

Grice's Clearfield Community Museum: 110, 111, 112 Patricia A. Mitchell.

Horseshoe Curve: 115 Therese Boyd. **117** Altoona Railroaders Memorial Museum.

Houdini Tour and Show: 8 Courtesy Houdini Tour and Show. **9** Rich Engel/Image Productions.

The Insectarium: 40, 41 Courtesy The Insectarium.

Jimmy Stewart Museum: 147 Courtesy Jimmy Stewart Museum. **148** Therese Boyd.

John Brown Museum: 165 Donna Coburn.

The Johnstown Flood Museum: 122 Pennsylvania State Archives.

Kready's Country Store Museum: 87 Rich Engel/Image Productions.

Le Petit Museum of Musical Boxes: 91, 92 Rich Engel/Image Productions.

Lost Highways Archive and Research Museum: 46 Courtesy Lost Highways.

Mattress Factory: 153 Courtesy Mattress Factory.

Moravian Pottery and Tile Works: 49, 50 Joe Pizarchik.

Mr. Ed's Elephant Museum: 125 Rich Engel/Image Productions. **126** Courtesy Mr. Ed's Elephant Museum.

Mummers Museum: 53 Courtesy Mummers Museum. **54** Urban Archives, Temple University Libraries.

Museum of Mourning Art: 58, 59 Ed Mazeika.

The New Holland Band Museum: 95 Rich Engel/Image Productions.

Ole Bull Museum: 184 Therese Boyd. **185** Tony Sanfilippo. **186** Joe Pizarchik.

Pasto Agricultural Museum: 129 Photo by Nabil K. Mark, Courtesy *Centre Daily Times*, State College.

Pennsylvania Lumber Museum: 189 Courtesy Pennsylvania Lumber Museum, Pennsylvania Historical and Museum Commission. **190** Pennsylvania State Archives.

Photo Antiquities: 156, 157, 158 Courtesy Photo Antiquities.

Piper Aviation Museum: 193, 194 Therese Boyd.

Richard Allen Museum: 62 Courtesy Mother Bethel A.M.E. Church. **63** Urban Archives, Temple University Libraries.

Rockhill Trolley Museum: 132 Therese Boyd.

Shoe Museum: 66, 67, 68 Courtesy The Shoe Museum, Temple University School of Podiatric Medicine, Philadelphia.

Tom Mix Birthplace and Museum: 196 Terese Boyd. **197** Tony Sanfilippo.

Toy Robot Museum: 99, 100 Rich Engel/Image Productions.

Vocal Groups Hall of Fame and Museum: 168 Courtesy Daniel R. Clemson and The Mills Brothers Society, Mechanicsburg.

Wharton Esherick Museum: 70, 71 Courtesy Wharton Esherick Museum.

White Christmas Chalet and Tree Farm: 12 Rich Engel/Image Productions.

Wild West Museum: 173 From the collection of Tony and Mary Pizarchik. **174** Therese Boyd.

Yuengling Brewery: 16 Courtesy Yuengling Beer Company.

Zane Grey Museum: 21 From Zane Grey's West Society website: http://www.zanegreysws.org/zgwestbk.htm. **22** Courtesy Zane Grey's West Society.

Zippo Case Museum: 200 Steven Mahon.

Library of Congress Cataloging-in-
Publication Data

Boyd, Therese.
The best places you've never seen :
Pennsylvania's small museums :
a traveler's guide / Therese Boyd.
p.   cm.
"A Keystone book."
ISBN 0-271-02276-0 (pbk. : alk. paper)
1. Museums—Pennsylvania—
Guidebooks.
2. Pennsylvania—Guidebooks.
I. Title.

AM12.P4 B69 2003
069'.09748—dc21

                          2002153322

BOOK DESIGN BY Regina Starace

It is the policy of The Pennsylvania
State University Press to use acid-free
paper. Publications on uncoated stock
satisfy the minimum requirements of
American National Standard for
Information Sciences—Permanence of
Paper for Printed Library Material, ANSI
Z39.48–1992.